world religions

by

Dorothy Arnett Dixon, Ph.D.

TWENTY-THIRD PUBLICATIONS
POST OFFICE BOX 180 WEST MYSTIC, CONN. 06388

This book has been adapted from the complete resource program book entitled *World Religions for the Classroom* by the same author (copyright 1975 by Twenty-Third Publications).

Library of Congress Catalog Card Number 77-002106

Printed in the United States of America.

Contents

This book is dedicated to Arthur Roy Dixon, Sr., my husband and sharer of interest in world religions.

Acknowledgments

This book, and the curriculum of which it is a part, is the product of many hands and many spirits. It has evolved over a period of years during which I have had the opportunity to share thoughts on world religions with students ranging in age from three to 80. Each time I have gone over these topics with others, I have gained from their reactions, questions, and suggestions. No student has gone through this curriculum without adding something, even if the addition was only an injection of enthusiasm. Some students have come forth with stories from their own religious lives which in turn have become an integral part of the curriculum. To all, I am grateful.

My earliest debt of gratitude is owed to two teachers who first taught the rudiments of this course at Webster College School in St. Louis County, Missouri, in the spring of 1968. Their names are Mrs. Mary Ann Salsich and Mrs. Miriam Meligrito Granger. My next debt of gratitude is to Mr. David Hohman who, as a field work student from Eden Theological Seminary in St. Louis, helped me go through some of these learning experiences with children in upper elementary grades during Saturday morning classes at St. John United Church of Christ in St. Charles, Missouri.

The third time around with this course was with junior high students at that same church, in a summer program which was entirely voluntary for the community. Mrs. Jane Bishop and Miss Mary Wepprich were my co-teachers for that experience which began with 21 students and ended with 31. Somehow, the program gained momentum as word got around that meaningful and interesting things were happening.

Then came adult courses, first at New Life School in St. Charles County; then at Eden Theological Seminary in Webster Groves, Missouri, at a Dialogue series which I co-taught with Dr. Allen O. Miller, and for which we had as resource persons Mr.

and Mrs. Nelkupaputhen Varghese John and Mrs. Ming Chen Liao Keller. Dr. Miller has been my teacher, advisor, and model for many years. Also, I have taught this course at Washington University Evening College and at the University of Missouri at St. Louis, in a summer workshop for public school teachers for two consecutive summers. During a course on Curriculum and Methods at Eden Theological Seminary this year, my students were quite helpful in making suggestions on both this book and its resource pages.

I am also thankful to a number of persons who have read chapters of my manuscript to verify my accuracy. The three chapters on Eastern religions have been read and corrected by Dr. Peter Gowing, Professor of World Religions at Southeast Asia Graduate School, whose home is in Singapore. The chapter on Judaism has been read and corrected by Rabbi Bernard Lipnick and Rabbi Arnold Asher of St. Louis, Missouri. Judith Herschlag Muffs, Director of Religious Curriculum for the Anti-Defamation League of B'nai B'rith offered invaluable assistance through her thorough criticism and suggestions. The chapter on Christianity has been read and approved by Sister Mary Byles of the faculty of Maryville College of the Sacred Heart, St. Louis County, Missouri, and by the Reverend Theodore G. Matkin, pastor of Marvin Park United Methodist Church, St. John, Missouri. The chapter on Islam has been read and corrected by Imam Dr. R.A. Khalifa of St. Louis, Missouri. I am grateful to each of these persons for reading, evaluating, and correcting my manuscript.

I also wish to thank Mr. Prem Bahl of India for advice on the Glossary and the resource pages and Ms. Barbara Corr for advice on Glossary pronunciation.

I wish also to acknowledge the cooperation above and beyond the call of duty of my publisher, Mr. Neil Kluepfel, who first encouraged me to prepare these materials for publication. As the project has progressed, he and his wife, Pat, have kept in constant communication with me, reading, evaluating, and suggesting ways of making the final product "come alive."

To my husband and four children who relinquished time I might have spent for them with broom and mop, I also offer sincere thanks. My husband, Arthur Roy Dixon, Sr., accompanied me in many travels when we visited churches, synagogues, Buddhist temples, Confucian temples, Shinto shrines, and many other places of worship. His warm and cordial manner helped us make friends with pastors, rabbis, and clergy of many faiths. My daughter, Dottie, began her introduction to world religions in one of my classes, but has since gone on to take courses at Northeast Missouri State University, and has provided me with new resources for pictures and quotations. My son, Arthur III, not only carried projectors, tape recorders, wall hangings, statues, and maps to dozens of classrooms for me, but became so interested in the subject that I came to count on him as assistant teacher. And my twins, Becky and Beth, have been the evaluators of interest-level for learning projects. Now in the sixth grade, they often spend time working through projects designed for this curriculum—producing symbols, ink-brush drawings, haiku poems, and statues for the "Durga Puga," not because they are asked to do it but because the materials are spread across my two desks and they latch on to every bit of available spare paper to engage in the learning experiences that they now consider fun.

To my typist, Mrs. Judi Brigham, I owe thanks for far more than merely the copying of the manuscript. It has been both her interest in the subject matter and her diligent pursuit of manuscript perfection that have kept me "on my toes"

In the final analysis, I accept full responsibility for all that is said in these chapters and in the accompanying packets. Yet as the work emerges full bloom, I realize how much a corporate effort it is, and how much it is an inspiration from Him Who, though addressed by many names and worshipped in many ways and in many languages, remains, as the theologian Paul Tillich affirmed, the Ground of all Being.

Dorothy A. Dixon

Preface

In a book entitled *World Religions* we need to be willing to define our use of the term, "religion." *Webster's New Twentieth Century Dictionary* shows the derivation of the word from the Latin, *re* (*back*) and *ligare* (*to bind together*). Thus in a basic definition of the word we consider its meaning in terms of relationships in which persons are bound with one another and with the Source of all being. Religion, in its broadest sense, then becomes the way people relate themselves individually and corporately to the Ultimate or supreme meaning in their lives. The *re* or "back" in the etymology gives reference to the estrangements that become reconciled as persons are "bound back."

Naturally, in different cultures, or among people of differing dispositions within cultures, there will be differences in the way the Ultimate is considered. Differing beliefs, behaviors, practices, and rituals are all a part of the cultural pluralism that undergirds civilization. Thus the Ultimate Source and Goal, generically termed God in the English language, is addressed by many different proper names in many differing languages and religious systems.

Yet there is a recognized universalism of religion. Hans-Joachim Schoeps, in *The Religions of Mankind* states,"Wherever men live on earth, religion springs into being. The science of religion encounters the fact that nowhere on earth have peoples been found who do not possess a religion . . . . " (pg.6) Joachim Wach, in *Types of Religious Experience, Christian and Non-Christian*, cites four universal criteria by which religious experience can be recognized. First, he says, it "is a response to what is experienced as ultimate reality." Second, it "is a total response of the total being to what is apprehended." Third, it "is the most intense experience of which man is capable;" and fourth, it "involves an imperative, a commitment which impels man to act." (*pp. 32-33*)

We have spoken of religion in general. We have also implied that there are many particular religions. Each particular religion usually includes a basic underlying philosophy and a set of beliefs and creeds, a code of ethics or guidelines to moral behavior, a value system, and many practices of observance, celebration, rite, and ritual. Worship of and praises to the Ultimate Creator-Sustainer, and prayers for aid are usually a part of religious practices. Such values as love, trust, joy, peacefulness, and forgiveness are often a part of religious orientations.

A frequent concomitant to religion is the whole area of magic and superstition. Yet there is a vast difference between religion and this realm. Religion, by another definition, is mankind's effort to get its will in accordance with the will of the Divine; magic and superstition are efforts to bend the will of the Divine into accordance with the wishes of humans. Although it is difficult and sometimes impossible to separate the religious from the magical aspects of a culture, this book concentrates totally on the religious practices and beliefs.

It would not be possible here to describe all of the world's religions. Those which claim the largest numbers of followers are given emphasis herewith. Also, the religions described in this book are the ones operative in modern times. No attempt is made to describe those of past centuries with influences which are minimal today. Apologies are offered for the omissions which a book of this size necessitates. Perhaps teachers using these curriculum materials can fill in areas which they want to cover by using approaches similar to the ones taken here – including objective presentations, multi-sensory experiences and the relation of the religions to art forms such as stories, poems, music, painting, dance and special celebrations.

D.A.D.

Introduction

The twentieth century began in a disjointed world of narrow provincialisms and inter-cultural suspicions. Some recent developments give hope that this same century may see the time when mutual understanding and appreciation will prevail across the lines of various religions and cultures. It is the goal of this book to aid in this process of mutual understanding, by delineating learning experiences that will acquaint students with the major worldwide faiths.

Early in the century, some scholars dreamed of finding the "common denominator" for these beliefs, and devising one world religion that would be acceptable to all persons. This idea came at a time when the dominant goal was a universalism that would be a sort of "melting pot' for all cultures. But the attempt brought forth such a "watered-down" version of religion that it seemed too weak to be acceptable to anyone. The writer, George Santayana, early in this century, noted:

> "The attempt to speak without speaking any particular language is not more hopeless than to have a religion that shall be no religion in particular. . . . Every living and healthy religion has a marked idiosyncrasy. Its power consists in its plural and surprising message and in the bias which that revelation gives to life." *Reason in Religion, 1905, Chapter 1.*

Santayana was saying that the religious pluralism which has been integral to mankind from the beginning of civilization continues to serve the differing needs of peoples in their relationships to God. Thus, the "melting pot" thrust of the early 1900's has now been replaced by a recognition of cultural pluralism, with concerted effort to enable persons to shed their suspicions and to engage in inter-faith dialogue.

What happens when persons learn of other religions? It is true that some facets of the differing cultures will take on real meaning for the learners. But it is also true that as students learn of how others worship, they develop a "mind set" for the importance of religion in general, and then they return to their own particular ways with renewed interest. Growth actually takes place in two dimensions: in the breadth of understanding of others and in the depth of a re-examination of the learner's own faith.

Dorothy Arnett Dixon teaches world religion courses at University College of Washington University (St. Louis), "Creative Activities for Children" at Forest Park Community College, and conducts a summer workshop, "Values, Religions, and Schools" at the University of Missouri, St. Louis.

She was director of Eden Laboratory School and is on the part-time faculty of Eden Theological Seminary. Her academic degrees include B.A., M.A., B.D. (with a major in systematic theology), and Ph.D. in education with a minor in sociology.

Mrs. Dixon is a member of the National Council in Religion and Public Education. She has written the curriculum Growth In Love and is author of the new preschool program The Formative Years published by Twenty-Third Publications.

She resides with her family in St. John, Missouri.

Hinduism

A meaningful study of India would be impossible without an introduction to Hinduism. This major world religion is the background upon which the whole culture of India rests. Native to the country of India and for the most part contained within that country, Hinduism reflects the meaning of life for more than 477 million people. It began more than 4,000 years ago when bards along the Indus River sang chants that were later written down as the Vedas, which are now part of the sacred literature of this religion. The name "Hindu" is derived from "Indus."

Thou Art God

One of the world's most diligent scholars of world religions, Dr. Wilfred Cantwell Smith, in a book called *The Faith of Other Men*, states that the most important belief of Hinduism can be summed up in one Sanscrit phrase: *Tat tuam asi*, meaning "That thou art." The first word of this phrase, "That" is a pronoun often used for God in Hinduism. God is thought of in this religion as the living force behind all of the universe, and is considered to be not only the Creator, but also the Creation. The holy name Brahman is used to designate God in Hinduism, but Brahman is considered not so much a personal entity as the name for Ultimate Reality or all that there is in the whole universe.

In Western thinking, persons refer to God as "He," and consider Him to be a personal entity, the Creator, but separate from His creation. The use of the pronoun "That" in Hindu thought is significant to explain a more mystical concept of the deity as a living and moving force within all things and all of life. Although some Hindus occasionally call upon Brahman personally, the basic tenet of Hinduism remains in the concept of God as Creator and Creation. *That* is ever the source and the goal of life in India.

Having glimpsed the Hindu concept of divinity as "That," let us move on to the second word of the phrase "That thou art." "Thou" is a designation for a human being who, in Hindu thought, is not only a part of Creation but also a part of the Creator, since the two are One. The word for the soul of man in Hindu culture is *atman*, but since all of the universe, including the soul of each living creature, is considered divine, it follows logically that the Hindu should consider each *atman* to be a part of the divine Soul. Hence, the third word of the phrase *Tat tuam asi* is a form of the verb "to be."

A more loose translation of *Tat tuam asi* would be "Thou art God." Imagine saying to a person in the Western Hemisphere "You are God." Imagine the uncomfortable reactions that would follow, because Western minds tend to think of Creator and creation as separate. Yet no Hindu feels presumptuous in seeing each person as God – the mystic view of life that pervades Hindu thought is the typical monastic affirmation that all is One, including even the smallest particle of creation.

An example of the one-ness felt in Hindu theology came through to this writer some years ago. I was sitting on a park bench with a young Hindu student from India, when the student became noticeably silent and immersed in thought. After a few moments, however, the student commented with a depth of feeling "Do you see that tree? That tree and I are one. We are the same. We may look different, but beneath all appearances, we are made of the same stuff, and a common soul unites us." I have remembered these words over the years because they seem to summarize the mystic Hindu spirit of unity in all things.

If one wonders how to explain the imperfections in human life, so different from the perfection which is divinity, there is the term *maya* which designates all the foibles and follies of mankind that cover up the divine spark deep within each human soul. *Maya* is a term for the world we see, the appearance of which is deceiving. Thus, *atman*, the human soul, is obscured by layers of *maya* so that it is quite difficult for anyone to recognize the soul of Brahman which dwells therein. Nevertheless, the basic Hindu affirmation comes through sharply and clearly in the phrase "Atman is Brahman" which is another way of saying "That thou art."

Mystic thought which is basic to Hindu thinking is best understood here as a way of considering all the universe as One. It is poetically described in the following verse from a Hindu scripture, the *Svetasvatara Upanishad*:

> "O Brahman Supreme!
> Formless art thou, and yet
> (though the reason none knows)
> Thou bringest forth many forms;
> Thou bringest them forth, and then
> Withdrawest them to thyself.
> Fill us with thoughts of thee!
>
> Thou art the fire,
> Thou art the sun,
> Thou art the air,
> Thou art the moon,
> Thou art the starry firmament,
> Thou art Brahman Supreme:
> Thou art the waters – thou,
> The creator of all!
>
> Thou art woman, thou art man,
> Thou art the youth, thou art the maiden,
> Thou art the old man tottering on his staff;
> Thou facest everywhere.
>
> Thou art the dark butterfly,
> Thou art the green parrot with red eyes,
> Thou art the thunder cloud, the seasons, the seas.
> Without beginning art thou,
> Beyond time, beyond space. . . . "(*Stace, 1960, pg. 44f.*)

Notice how this exquisite poem sings of Brahman as *being* his creation. In the poem, Brahman *is* the fire, the sun, the air, the moon, the starry firmament, the waters, the woman, the man. . . . Brahman is celebrated as both Creator and Creation. In a similarly inspirational hymn from Western literature, we see a parallel celebration of the Creator, but a contrast in that the elements of creation stand apart in praise:

"All creatures of our God and King,
Lift up your voice and with us sing
Alleluia, Alleluia!
Thou burning sun with golden beam,
Thou silver moon with softer gleam,
O praise him, O praise him,
Alleluia, Alleluia, Alleluia.

Thou rushing wind that art so strong,
Ye clouds in heaven that sail along,
O praise him, Alleluia!
Thou rising morn in praise rejoice,
Ye lights of evening find a voice,
O praise him, O praise him,
Alleluia, Alleluia, Alleluia.

Thou flowing water, pure and clear,
Make music for thy lord to hear,
Alleluia, Alleluia, Alleluia.
Thou fire so masterful and bright,
That givest man both warmth and light,
O praise him, O praise him,
Alleluia, Alleluia, Alleluia!

And all ye men of tender heart,
Forgiving others take your part,
O sing ye, Alleluia!
Ye who long pain and sorrow bear,
Praise God and on him cast your care
O praise him, O praise him,
Alleluia, Alleluia, Alleluia!

St. Francis of Assisi

Both hymns have the sun, moon, clouds, fire, men, and many other elements in eloquent relation to their Creator. But in the Hindu hymn, these elements are inextricably a part of their Creator, whereas in the hymn by St. Francis the elements stand distinct from the Creator and are called to praise him. Perhaps these two masterpieces of devotional literature sum up the basic difference of viewpoint between India and the West.

The "Exceptions that Prove the Rule"

In pointing out this distinction between the monism of Hindu thought and creature-Creator theology in Western religions, we do *not* mean to say that "East is East and West is West and never the twain shall meet." We speak in appreciation for the variety of insights. Furthermore, we need to point out that there are a number of exceptions to the basic concepts of both East and West. For instance in Western literature, there are a number of mystic writings, such as the writings of Meister Eckhart and St. Bonaventura which have as their goal the realization of man's one-ness with God. Also, there are the writings from the Jewish school of Hasidism. Conversely, in Eastern thought, there are Bhakti yogis who insist that man must stand apart from God in order to love God. An example of this kind of poetry is found in the Song of Tukaram in *An Indian Peasant Mystic*:

"Can water quaff itself?
Can trees taste of the fruit they bear?
He who worships God must stand distinct from Him,
So only shall we know the joyful love of God;
For if he say that God and he are one,
That joy, that love, shall vanish instantly away.

Pray no more for utter oneness with God:
Where were the beauty if jewel and setting were one?
The heat and the shade are two,
If not, where were the comfort of shade?
Mother and child are two,
If not, where were love?
When after long being sundered, they meet,
What joy do they feel, the mother and child!
Where were joy if the two were one?
Pray, then, no more for utter oneness with God."

(*Smith, 1958, pp. 40-41*)

This poem is an exception to the Hindu affirmation that "Atman is Brahman" or "Thou art God." If it is an exception that "proves the rule," it is also an entree for inter-faith dialogue.

One God, many Forms

To a traveler passing through India, Hinduism might appear to be a religion of many gods. For instance, the traveler might meet some Hindus who call upon God by the name of Vishnu, and others praying to Shiva. There are numerous pilgrimages and festivals in India for these deities. But in Hindu theology, Vishnu and Shiva are merely aspects of one God, Brahman. Actually, Brahman is considered to be manifest in a trinity of names: Brahma, the Creator; Vishnu, the Preserver; and Shiva, the Destroyer. To Christians who are used to referring to one God in a trinity of names, this trinitarian aspect of Hinduism may not be surprising. The three names for the phases of Brahman are proliferated, however, by many more divine names, as each person of the Hindu trinity is considered matched to a mate who represents some other phase of existence; and each of the "gods" is housed in a temple or shrine where devotees "bathe, feed, and honor them."

In addition to the plethora of names for divinity in India, there are also names for the *avatara* or incarnations of God, such as Rama and Krishna who are considered to be Vishnu appearing in human form. In the sacred literature called the *Bhagavad Gita*, the "*Song of God*," *avataras* or incarnations are explained as Vishnu sings through Krishna:

> "When goodness grows weak,
> When evil increases,
> I make myself a body.
>
> In every age I come back
> To deliver the holy,
> To destroy the sin of the sinner.
> To establish righteousness." (*Pg. 50*)

Swami Satprakashananda of the Vedanta Society of St. Louis, Missouri, once said to this writer: "Hinduism and Christianity have much in common, because we both believe that God is personal enough to visit earth in human form. The difference lies in the number of incarnations in Hinduism as opposed to the one in Christianity."

A traveler in India might also wonder why Shiva, the destroyer phase of God, is worshipped so often. In Western thought, we tend to minimize or gloss over the topic of death. But in Hindu thought, death is but a gateway to a new life, through the process called reincarnation or transmigration. In this process, the soul is considered to be born again and again into different bodies, so that the cycle of birth, life, death, and rebirth is considered normative. This cycle is called *samsara.*

In *samsara*, the soul is believed to be reborn into a new station of life according to its deeds in the previous life. Thus by the law of *karma*, which is the law of cause and effect, a soul who has lived a good and noble life will be reborn, after death, into a situation of higher esteem. Contrariwise, the soul could be born in a lower state if the deeds of the previous life had been predominately evil. A person at the bottom rung of the highly stratified Indian society, who lived an evil life, would theoretically be reborn into an animal according to the law of *karma*. Transmigration is a term for a soul passing from the human to lower forms of life, or *vice versa*.

From the *Bhagavad Gita* we read the following poetic description of *samsara*:

> "Worn-out garments
> Are shed by the body:
> Worn-out bodies
> Are shed by the dweller
> Within the body.
> New bodies are donned
> By the dweller, like garments." (Pg. 37)

This cycle of birth, life, death, and rebirth is not, however, considered to be futile, like the grinding of a wheel that never stops. The purpose of the many lifetimes is the goal of perfection, so that each soul has the chance to rise higher and higher in each lifetime. The soul, for instance, may come back to live in a person of a higher rung on the social ladder, provided it deserves such promotion. The social ladder in India is made up of castes, the lowest being the Sudras or laborers and just above the Sudras the Vaisyas or overseers. The Kshatriya caste is next, composed of warriors and administrators. At the top of the social ladder are the Brahmins or seers and priests. Note that this name for the highest class is Brahm*in*, not to be confused with Brahm*an*, the name for God.

If a soul has already attained Brahmin status and lives a life of good deeds, then upon death it does not need to be reborn, but merges indistinguishably with the soul of God in a condition called *moksha* or *mukti*. Thus the goal of all of Hindu life has been reached, through a countless number of births and rebirths, and in each lifetime, meticulous attention to *dharma*, the duties and rituals of the castes.

Sacred Symbols

This upward progression of the *atman* or human soul is symbolized by the lotus flower which, too, rises out of the earth to become a thing of beauty. Indeed, the entire Hindu religion is represented in the symbol of the lotus blossom.

Another symbol often used in this religion is the *OM*, made up of three Sanscrit letters that sum up the godhead. Often in Hindu worship, this sacred symbol *OM* is pronounced with great fervor – so that the wind from the lungs is like the spirit of God coming forth. The *OM* sound combines all the fullness of the vocal sounds, because it begins at the back of the throat with an "au" sound, proceeds to the palate with an "o" sound, and ends with the labial "m" sound. It thus expresses the completeness of the call to God with the fullness of sound and soul.

Yogas and Yogis

To help the individual rise through the stations of life, there are certain disciplines in Hinduism, and these are called *yogas*. Actually the word yoga comes from the word for "yoke," which means to join together in concerted effort. Since people differ in their aptitudes in life, there are various *yogas* or ways to strive. For the person intellectually oriented, there is *Jnana yoga*, the realization of God through thinking, listening, and knowledge. For the person of a more emotional nature, *Bhakti yoga* is the way to God through utter devotion. *Karma yoga* is the discipline of realizing God through good deeds, done in private without praise or other reward. Finally, there is *Ra ja yoga* which is a concerted effort to realize God through such spiritual exercises as body posture, breath control, and meditation which goes into the depths of the inner self. Persons who diligently and systematically seek to perfect their one-ness with God through any of these disciplines are called *yogis*. Some *yogis* concentrate so arduously that they are caught up in a rapture called *samhadi* which means literally "one-ness with God."

A young man from India recently told a class of college students in America about a *yogi* he knew who would go into *samhadi* frequently. When he was in *samhadi* his pulsebeat and breathing would be so faint that he would appear to be lifeless. In one of these trances, this *yogi* was taken to a mortuary by persons who had found him and believed him to be dead. In actuality, the *yogi* was very much alive, and came out of *samhadi* just in time to prevent his own funeral!

We have learned a number of words such as *samsara* (the cycle of life, death, and rebirth), and *samhadi* (the realization of one-ness of the soul with God). Let's learn one more before we proceed to ways of teaching this religion in a classroom. The final word is *sanyasi*. The *Sanyasi* is a person in the fourth stage of a lifetime, in the culmination of his years. Thus, for each person there are four stages of life: the student phase, the householder phase, the retirement phase, and finally that period after retirement that is the *sanyasi* phase. The *sanyasi* is finally free from the material burdens of life – from all cares and from all responsibilities. He is free to wander, without possessions, begging bowl in hand, and to concentrate on his one-ness with God. The *maya* or illusion of life that obscures the real self is at a minimum for the *sanyasi*, who is unburdened and liberated. There is a drama about a *sanyasi* in the resource pages for this section.

Though the Hindu way of life is socially rigid in its caste system, it is philosophically one of the most liberal of all religions. Lacking the narrow provincialisms of many Western sects, the Hindu spirit affirms, "The various religions are but the many languages through which God has spoken to the human heart." (Smith, 1958, pg. 85)

Sects which Grew from Hinduism

In India, there are a number of sects which grew from Hinduism, particularly the Jains and the Sikhs. The Jains, descendents of followers of Mahivira (599-527 B.C.) are best known for their austere reverence for life, and for nonviolence. So insistent is their determination not to harm life, that many of the Jains wear veils to keep them from accidently breathing in an insect. They would not kill a mosquito even if it were biting them.

Jains often carry brooms to sweep their paths so they will not step on insects. They often support beast hospitals for sick buffaloes, cows, goats, or sheep. Sacred scriptures of the Jains are the *Agamas*, sermons of Mahavira. Some Jains wear white robes; others wear nothing.

Sikhs are a much younger sect, begun in the fifteenth century A.D. by the followers of Nanak. Nanak was born into a family of Vishnu worshippers, and he practiced Bhakti devotion. But he became influenced by Muslims who had come to India and who were in opposition to the Hindus. After listening to spokesmen from both religions, Nanak founded Sikhism which is a syncretism of Hinduism and Islam, yet with a theology of its own. Sacred scripture is the *Granth* completed by Arjun, the fifth guru. Sikhs wear their hair long, usually dress in blue robes, and are not opposed to fighting.

Both Jains and Sikhs oppose the caste system in India and there are over 2,000,000 Jains and over 4,500,000 Sikhs in the country today.

A Jain on a roadside in India.

Somnath Temple, Gujarat.

Discussion Questions on Hinduism

1. If a Hindu were to say to a friend: "You are God," what would he mean?
2. What basic difference is there between Hindu theology and most Western theologies? Is the difference absolute?
3. How does Hindu theology explain human imperfections? What is *maya*?
4. Why is there such a place of reverence in Hindu theology for the destroyer form of God? In other words, what is the Hindu attitude toward death?
5. What would you say is the ultimate goal of life in Hinduism? How do *karma* and reincarnations help obtain this goal?
6. Would you consider Hinduism to be monotheistic or polytheistic? Explain.
7. If you were a Hindu yogi, would you be a gnana (realizing God through knowledge) yogi, a karma (realizing God through deeds) yogi, a bhakti (realizing God through love) yogi, or a raja (realizing God through spiritual exercises) yogi? In other words, do you see yourself as basically a thinking, a doing, a loving, or a methodically disciplined person?
8. What parallels to the caste system do you see in your own culture?
9. What is the Hindu attitude toward other religions?
10. What two major world religions believe that God has come to earth in human form to guide mankind?

OM, the most sacred word for Hindus

Bibliography on Hinduism

A. **Books:**

(It is suggested that there be a "browsing table" in the classroom):

Sacred literature:

The Bhagavad-Gita translated by Swami Prabhavananda and Christopher Isherwood, New York: (A Mentor Book) 1954.

The *Upanishads* (available in paperback from Harper Torchbooks, translated by Swami Nikhilananda in 1963 or in Penguin Classics, translated by Juan Mascaro in 1965).

The Ramayana and *The Mahabharata* New York: Everyman's Library, 1920.

Other books (See also general reference list):

Basham, A.L. *The Wonder that was India.* New York: Grove Press, 1954.

Dasi, K.D. and S.D. *The Hare Krishna Cook Book.* New York: The Bhaktivedanta Book Trust, 1973.

Fischer, Louis. *Ghandi, His Life and Message for the World.* New York: Signet Books, 1954.

Levai, Blaise. *Ask an Indian about India.* New York: Friendship Press, 1972.

Nivedita, Sister. *Cradle Tales of Hinduism.* Calcutta: Aduaita Ashrama, 1972. (Can be bought from Vedanta Society, 205 S. Skinker, St. Louis, Mo. 63105).

Pitt, Malcolm. *Introducing Hinduism.* New York: Friendship Press, 1955.

Radhakrishnan, S. *The Hindu View of Life.* London: Unwin Books, 1960. Also published by The Macmillan Co., Riverside Drive, New Jersey.

Renou, Louis. *Hinduism.* New York: Simon and Schuster, 1961.

Rice, Edward. *Mother India's Children.* New York: Friendship Press, 1972.

Sethi, Narendra. *Hindu Proverbs.* Mount Vernon, New York: Peter Pauper Press, 1962.

Tagore, Rabindranath. *Collected Poems and Plays.* New York: The Macmillan Company, 1952.

Van Horne, M. *Come Inside India.* New York: Friendship Press, 1972.

Wells, Irene. *Fun and Festival from India, Pakistan, Ceylon, Nepal.* New York: Friendship Press.

White, Emmons. *The Wisdom of India.* Mount Vernon, New York: Peter Pauper Press, 1968.

Wood, Ernest. *Concentration, An Approach to Meditation.* Wheaton, Ill.: The Theosophical Publishing House, 1949.

B. **Audio Visuals:**

Filmstrips:

"Hinduism" from series *The World's Great Religions.* New York: *Time-Life* Filmstrips.

"Hinduism" from series *Religions of our World Neighbors.* Family Filmstrips.

Films:

"Major Religions of the World." Encyclopedia Britannica (B&W) 20 minutes, 1954.

"The Hindu World." Coronet Films, 65 E. South Water St., Chicago 60601.

Part I of "Four Religions" narrated by Arnold Toynbee. New York: McGraw-Hill.

Records:

"Listening in on India." New York: Friendship Press, 1972.

"Mantras." Songs of Yoga, Swami Sivananda-Radha Ashram: Yasodhara Ashram; Kootenay Bay, B.C., Canada.

Bhattacharya, D. "Religions of India." The Living Tradition, Decca Record Co., Ltd., Argo Division.

"Every Town and Village." New York: Bhaktivedanta Book Trust, 1972.

"Chants and Prayers." Paramahansa Yogananda Self-Realization Fellowship (3880 San Raphael Ave., Los Angeles, Calif. 90065).

Pictures:

Rice, Edward. *Photo Sutra.* New York: Friendship Press, 1972.

India's Gods and Kings. School Picture Set 8, Metropolitan Museum of Art, New York City 10028.

Game:

Hindu Pyramid Puzzle, World Wide Games, Box 450, Delaware, Ohio 43015 (order WWG135, Price $3.95).

Buddhism

Buddhism grew out of Hinduism through the founding figure of Siddhartha Gautama who came to be known as the Buddha, or Enlightened One. Though born in India, Buddhism is not widely practiced there today, but flourishes instead in other parts of Asia numbering more than 267 million followers. The form which Buddhism takes differs in southeast Asia from the form it takes in northern Asia, yet both forms have their common ancestry in the historic figure of Siddhartha Gautama. Let us glimpse his life story which, though overlaid with legend as in the case of most great men, has its basis in actual history.

Story of the Buddha

About the year 560 B.C., a son, Siddhartha Gautama, was born to the ruler of one of the provinces of northern India. Legend has it that seven wise men from the hills came to visit the ruler, and announced that the new baby was so remarkable that he was certain to become a leader of men. "If he stays with the world," they proclaimed, "he will be king of all of India. But if he rejects the world, he will become a redeemer of mankind."

The king was more interested in seeing his son become king, so he did all in his power to keep the growing boy interested in worldly affairs. "I wore garments of silk and the attendants held a white umbrella over me" (Smith, 1958, pg. 91), Gautama later recalled of his childhood. As the boy grew older, his father provided him with three palaces and four thousand dancing girls. A marriage was arranged between Prince Gautama and a neighboring princess Yasodhara, and the wedded couple were later gifted with a son, Rahula.

In spite of royal commands that Gautama be shielded from all knowledge of suffering, at one point in his young life the prince made a startling discovery. One afternoon, while out riding with one of his servants, the young prince saw a man by the roadside. It was an old man with scraggly teeth and very thin hair who was so bent with age that he was resting on a cane. "Whatever is the matter with that man?" Gautama asked of his servant. The servant had to explain that the man was bent with age and that old age comes to all who live long years.

The next day the prince and his servant went riding again, and this time they beheld a man, wracked with illness, lying by the roadside, convulsing with fever. Again Gautama asked, out of deep concern, about the status of the man, and the servant replied that the man was stricken with sickness which comes to most persons in the course of a lifetime. The prince was greatly dismayed at the suffering he was seeing.

On the third day, the prince and his servant beheld a funeral cart carrying a corpse, and a woman and children walking behind it, crying. The young prince asked, and was told, about death. He was horrified to realize that death is something that comes, sooner or later, to everyone. He spent long hours pondering this third disclosure of suffering.

On the fourth day, prince Gautama and his servant beheld a monk, dressed in saffron robes, with his head shaven, and with a begging bowl in his hand. There was a look of serenity on the face of the monk, as if he had gone beyond the ways of the world and had come to grips with the problem of suffering. The prince realized that he, too, must renounce the world and somehow find answers to the riddle of life.

Thus, one night when he was twenty-nine years old, Siddhartha Gautama kissed his sleeping wife and son good-bye and departed for the forest for a life of renunciation and a search for the meaning of life and an answer to suffering. Halfway into the forest, he changed clothing with his servant and sent the servant back to the palace. By himself in the forest, Gautama felt the loneliness of solitude.

The six years in the forest that followed are divided into three periods: First, Gautama studied under Hindu hermits until he had learned all that they could teach. Then he tried asceticism – giving up all worldly pleasures and eating only one bean a day to keep alive. In this second period, Gautama became so thin that he could feel his spine by pressing upon his abdomen, and the dirt accumulated so thickly on his body that it could be scraped off in large hunks. Finally, he became so weak that he could no longer think, and if friends had not come to feed him some warm rice gruel, he surely would have died.

Gautama learned from this self-torture that too much deprivation was as harmful as too much luxury, and the beginning of his doctrine of "The Middle Way" was born. The five friends, who had been fasting with him, were disappointed that Gautama had given up their way of life, but he promised them that if he should ever find the answer to the problem of suffering and to the meaning of life, he would come back to them and share his discoveries.

The third phase of Gautama's life in the forest was *raja yoga*, deep meditation with special body position that is conducive to thought. At the culmination of this period, on one historic night of nights, Gautama sat down under a tree and vowed he would not rise again until he had found enlightenment. Through hour after hour, he sat in deeper and deeper meditation until – in the early hours of the dawn, as the tree rained red flowers and the earth quivered as in the pangs of childbirth, the seeker knew that at last he had been put in touch with the ultimate meaning of life. For 49 days, he sat in a trance at the foot of the tree, completely in awe of his experience. Then he arose, sought out his friends, and began to communicate the meaning he had found. From that point onward, Gautama was known as the Buddha, the "Enlightened One" and the tree under which he had found enlightenment was called the "Bo" or "Bodhi" tree.

What was the answer the Buddha had found? It is best seen in the actions of the rest of his life, during which for almost 50 years he traveled from village to village, ministering to each person in the way he needed help. To some, the Buddha became a listener; to others, he became a provider of food and shelter; some he gathered to himself as a band of disciples who could learn and minister with him. But all was done in a spirit of selfless compassion, and in a life midway between the extremes of luxury and poverty.

In one of his famous sermons to his followers, Buddha summarized his insight into the problem of suffering by delineating the "Four Noble Truths" and the "Eightfold Path." These will be discussed later. He also preached a way of life which, though based on his knowledge of Hinduism, denounced the caste system, scorned ritual, and ignored metaphysics. That is, the Buddha disclaimed speculation on the nature or essence of God, but bent all energies toward serving the needs of the world. His new philosophy is summed up in the parable of the man with an arrow in his back. The Buddha said that it is of no use to question who shot the arrow or where the shooter was standing but rather to bend all efforts on removing the arrow.

Finally, when the Buddha was more than 80 years old, he was invited to have dinner with a special friend by the name of Cunda. Cunda prepared mushrooms, the Buddha's favorite food. But, unknowingly, he prepared some which were poisonous. Soon the Buddha realized that he was dying.

On his deathbed, the Buddha summoned his followers and, determined to ease Cunda's anguish and guilt feelings, declared: "In all my lifetime, two meals stand out supreme: one was the meal that I ate before I sat under the Bo tree, after which I received enlightenment; the other, tonight, at the home of my dear friend, Cunda, after which I shall receive *Nirvana*." So saying, the Buddha breathed his last and passed into the eternal absence of pain, designated as *Nirvana*.

His followers gathered his sayings and sermons into the *Tripitaka*, or *Three Baskets of Wisdom*.

The Four Noble Truths and Eightfold Path

The Four Noble Truths which the Buddha proclaimed are meant to explain and alleviate the problem of suffering in life. The first truth is the recognition that "In life, suffering abounds." To gloss over the realities of life is not to come to grips with reality. The second truth is that "Suffering is caused by desire." As long as persons are determined to have unobtainable pleasures and possessions, they are faced with a continual round of disappointments. The third truth is that "The cure lies in overcoming selfish craving." To give up this insatiable thirst for pleasure and property is to eliminate suffering. When persons no longer expect a life of ease, they are no longer disappointed.

The fourth Noble Truth provides the way to achieve the life of non-desire, through the Eightfold Path. This Path consists of eight steps.

1. **Right knowledge.** The first step in liberation from suffering is knowing what causes men to suffer. As long as people yearn for some permanent, unchangeable state of existence, they are doomed to disappointment, because in life there is constant change. Life is impermanent, (*anicca*) and the man of right knowledge simply expects it to be this way.

2. **Right motives.** Knowing the truth about the impermanence of life, persons are then called to desire more obtainable objectives. Motives need to be based on values that benefit others instead of on building up one's own possessions. Kindness and love are true values, and the man whose motives are to express these virtues has met the requirements of the second step of the eightfold path.

3. **Right speech.** The person following the eightfold path can no longer engage in gossip or slander, or in talk that is crude and offensive. The speech of this person will be controlled, considerate, and thoughtful. Words can be hurtful or helpful, but the person of right speech chooses only those which are helpful.

4. Right action. Beyond what a person says is what he does. A person might speak with considerable kindness, but unless his deeds back up his words, he is "shouting down a rain barrel." A list of five actions that are absolutely unacceptable grew up and these prohibitions are phrased as follows:

Do not steal
Do not kill
Do not lie
Do not commit adultery
Do not drink intoxicants

But in addition to these acts that are forbidden, there are other acts that are required, such as listening to a person who wants to tell his problems, helping the hungry to find food, and helping the homeless to find shelter. Along with this call for helpful action, is also a call to refrain from counter-attacking those who wrong you. The man of right action refuses to get on the level of a person who is himself abusive, either in word or deed.

5. Right occupation. The Buddha recognized that some ways of making a living are hurtful ways and should not be permitted. Thus, he specifically forbade being a butcher, a caravan trader, a seller of poisons or dope, a slave trader or a slave owner. He also spoke against earning a living by the making or selling of liquors, or by being a professional soldier. Some persons began to believe that living as a monk in a monastery was the only really unhurtful way of life, but as the idea of Buddhism as a way of life for all people grew, it was seen that many good Buddhists are needed to live in everyday life outside the monastery. Yet, these persons need to choose their livelihood carefully so as to help, not hurt any living creature.

6. **Right perseverance.** Some persons start a way of life with great zest, but soon lag in interest. To meet the requirement of the sixth step in the eightfold path, a person must persist in his way of life, untiringly. This person must find the rate of effort that gives best results, and stick to it. This emphasis on right effort means not rushing so hard as to blunder, nor working so slowly as to drag, but to persevere consistently and effectively at the chosen tasks.

7. **Right awareness.** The person who has reached this seventh step on the path has learned to see things in perspective, objectively rather than subjectively. That is, this person is aware that no matter how much his senses cry out to him, he is bigger than his sensual self. The story is told that a monk was once asked if he had seen a lady pass his way, to which the monk replied: "I do not know if it was a lady or a man, but a set of bones is traveling this way." The person of right awareness sees life in its fullness not in the immediacy of the pangs of hunger, thirst, or lust.

8. **Right absorption.** The final step on the eightfold path is the culmination of all others. It means that the person is now ready to be absorbed into the infinite, being freed from all the limitations of a sensual existence.

According to Buddhist doctrine, when the self is rightly absorbed into one-ness with the infinite, it is ready for *Nirvana*. All cravings and desires, all attachment to self are extinguished, like a candle that goes out. Then the self is "soul-less" (*anatta*) and impermanent (*anicca*). Some Buddhists see *Nirvana* as a goal to self-extinction, and others as a goal to the extinction of all desires, but in either case, it is a description of a state of relief from the endless round of suffering that confronts the human race. In theory, one can enter *Nirvana* in this life and enter permanent *Nirvana* (*Parinirvana*) after death.

Theravada and Mahayana Buddhism

We mentioned earlier that Buddhism has taken different forms in different areas of Asia. In southeast Asia, in countries such as Burma, Ceylon, and Thailand, Theravada (also called Hinayana) Buddhism prevails. In this form of Buddhism, the goal of life is the salvation of each individual soul in order that each person can enter *Nirvana* by virtue of his own good works. Monks, called *arhats*, spend their lifetimes doing good works, caring for the temples or *stupas*, covering them with gold leaf or working in other constructive ways, in order to earn their way to *Nirvana*. The people of these areas prefer the title "Theravada" because it refers to honor of the vedas (scriptures and teachings from the Hindus). "Hinayana" means the "lesser vessel" and therefore sets this form of Buddhism in comparison with "Mahayana" of northern Asia.

"Mahayana" means the "greater .vessel," and refers to Buddhism in China, Japan, Korea, North Viet-Nam and South Viet-Nam. The Mahayana Buddhist is not as interested in individual salvation as in the good of all peoples, or social salvation. In Mahayana Buddhism, monks do not usually spend a lifetime in a monastery, but move freely among the people to be of help to all of society. Those who have attained readiness for *Nirvana* become *Bodhisattvas*, persons who refuse to accept Nirvana until all persons are ready for it. There is also a belief in Mahayana Buddhism that since persons cannot really *earn Nirvana*, they can be saved by faith in *Amida Buddha*, the spirit of the eternal Buddha, who grants grace to those who accept it. Thus, within Mahayana Buddhism, there are two concepts of Buddha: the historic Siddhartha Gautama, also known as "Sakyamuni," (meaning wise one from the Sakya tribe), and the eternal Amida Buddha, who grants grace to the faithful by enabling them to pass on to a "Pure Land" that leads to *Nirvana*.

Zen Buddhism

Mahayana Buddhism is divided into numerous sects, one of which deserves special attention here since many teaching activities are related to it. We refer now to Zen Buddhism, which is a form that abounds in Japan, having roots in the Chan Buddhism of China. In this form, the student seeks to reach enlightenment or *satori* not through intellectual endeavors but by way of an intuitive moment in which the truth breaks through. Zen monks spend years in rigid discipline, often working on monastery farms where their days are divided into periods of work and periods of meditation. In meditation, they seek to empty their minds of all distracting thoughts. Often they are goaded by instructors with *koans*, which are special puzzling questions that in their absurdity may lead to a flash of enlightenment. An example of a *koan* is: "What is the sound of the clapping of one hand?"

Their life harmonizes with the world of nature and earth, so that a simple and quiet austerity pervades the Zen monastery. Tea is the typical drink of Zen monks, because it keeps the mind alert in meditation. Legend has it that Bodhidharma, who first brought this strand of Buddhism from India to China, once cut off his eyelids because they kept drooping in drowsiness during meditation. In the legend, these eyelids fell to earth and the first tea plant sprang up from that spot.

The serving and drinking of tea is an art form in Zen Buddhism. Whenever a person performs the tea ceremony, there is quiet and rapt attention as the server moves with easy, graceful strokes to position the coals in the brazier, to dip the dry tea into the cups, ladle just the proper amount of boiling water, and whip the mixture into a frothy green foam. Participants are banded together in the solemnity and deep meaning of the special tea ceremony.

The surroundings of Zen meditation are artistic in their simplicity. One simple flower arrangement, often fashioned from only one flower, will grace the room. Zen gardens reflect a stark simplicity, and a moving beauty. Zen paintings are often ink-brush drawings done with a whirlwind effect of sudden inspiration. In contrast to labored masterpieces, these quick, intuitive flashes of inspiration are done with zestful spontaneity.

Even the jujitsu art of self-defense is related to Zen Buddhism. It abounds in relaxed, almost effortless movement that comes to a sudden and decisive thrust like the flash of *satori*.

Buddhist Religious Practices

In Mahayana Buddhism, each home has an altar with a picture or statue of a Buddha and a memorial tablet listing deceased members of the household. Every day devout Buddhists recite sutras (sacred literature) and place offerings of flowers, incense, tea, and cakes before the altar. "Grace" at the dinner table is spoken in the following Japanese words: "Itadakimasu" (for the beginning of the meal) and "Gochiso sama" (at the closing of the meal).

Special occasions are celebrated in communities, with festivals and parades. Buddha's birthday, April 8, is celebrated in temples where a flower shrine representing the newborn Sakyamuni is honored with tea. (A legend states that it rained tea the day the Buddha was born!) Children, dressed in special festive attire, bring flowers and ladle sweet tea over the replica of the newborn babe. Buddha's death day, February 15, is observed by his followers who make special offerings of cake, fruit, flowers, and incense before temple and home altars.

During the months of July and August in Japan, Buddhist temples hold the O-Bon Odori, a service in honor of the dead, especially those who have died in the previous year. Following a service in the temple, where incense is burned and scriptures are read, the congregation participates in an evening of dancing around an orchestra stand in the courtyard. The dancing is lilting and colorful, as dancers of all ages in bright kimonos move with precise and rhythmic steps, around and around the bandstand. At two other times in the year (spring and fall equinox) graves are cleaned, decorated, and honored.

In the Japanese Shin sects, thanksgiving services called *Hoonko*, last a week and are held in homes and temples. Weekly services of worship are held in many of these temples on Sunday mornings. Worshippers enter the *Hondo* (temple hall), go forward to the altar and *gasho* (bow), offer incense, then take their places in the congregation as the gong sounds and the priest reads scriptures and perhaps gives a sermon. Prayer beads (*ojuzu*) are used to encircle the hands, which are placed together during *gasho*.

A rapidly growing sect of Japanese Buddhism called Soka Gakkai combines traditional festivities with a white-uniformed marching discipline. Drums and fifes accentuate this newly-formed style of expression. Ironically, the tenets of the faith are strongly oriented toward world peace, yet the ritual practices give a highly militant appearance. The movement is both social and political, yet claims that its roots are in the ancient Buddhist tradition of Nichiren Shoshu.

Although priests and monks abound in Mahayana Buddhism, the emphasis throughout this culture is on the life of the lay person. Priests in many sects, especially Shin, marry and live in families. Although meditation, inner peace, and control of desires are stressed, the quality of living for the whole community is an active consideration. Many Buddhist temples offer programs in social service and helping others.

Theravada Buddhism, on the other hand, stresses the monastic life. A usual sight in the countries of southeast Asia is the Buddhist monk in saffron robe going from door to door at early morn with "begging bowl" in hand. Lay Buddhists give rice and other offerings to these monks in order to support them and to gain merit for themselves. Monasteries are centers for education, and serve the community in other ways, also, such as providing counseling and social life.

A ceremony basic to Buddhism is exemplified in the Burmese custom of *Shin Byu*, the dramatic re-enactment of Buddha's renunciation of worldly life. Young boys are prepared for the ceremony, dressed in princely clothes such as those worn by the prince Siddhartha Gautama. The whole community feasts to celebrate the occasion. Then the young boys take off the rich robes to don the saffron robes of the monks, and go off to live for weeks, months, or years in monasteries, just as the original Buddha rejected luxury for a life detached from worldly pleasure.

Kelaniya Temple, Sri-Lanka.

Two Japanese nuns, one a Buddhist, the other Roman Catholic, chat at an outdoor market.

Discussion Questions on Buddhism

1. What was Siddhartha Gautama seeking when he left his life of luxury?
2. What ways did he follow to find his answers? Describe his six years in the forest.
3. How would you have felt about him if you had been one of the persons he deserted when he gave up his period of fasting? (Have five persons "role play" the parts of the five friends he left.)
4. What truth did Siddhartha Gautama discover when fasting became as ineffectual as luxury?
5. Describe how it might have felt to be Siddhartha Gautama on that momentous night of enlightenment under the Bodhi tree.
6. What "way of life" followed the Buddha's enlightenment?
7. How could you sum up the essence of the Four Noble Truths and the Eightfold Path? In other words, tell these truths in your own words.
8. Describe *Nirvana* as you understand it.
9. Differentiate between Mahayana and Hinayana (Theravada) Buddhism.
10. What is the use of the *koan* in Zen Buddhism?

Bibliography on Buddhism

A. Books:

Beilenson, Peter, and Behn, Harry (Translators). *Haiku Harvest.* Mt. Vernon, New York: The Peter Pauper Press, 1962.

Davidson, Georgie. *Color Treasury of Japanese Flower Arranging.* New York: Crescent Books, 1973.

Gard, Richard. *Buddhism.* New York: Simon and Schuster, 1962.

Holmes, Stewart and Horioka, Chimyo. *Zen Art For Meditation.* Rutland, Vt.: Charles E. Tuttle Co., 1973.

Kapleau, Philip. *Three Pillars of Zen.* Boston: Beacon Press, 1967.

Latourette, K.S. *Introducing Buddhism.* New York: Friendship Press, 1959.

Reps, Paul. *Zen Flesh, Zen Bones.* Garden City, New York: Anchor Books (Doubleday).

Sakade, Florence. *Origami: Japanese Paper Folding*, Book 1. Rutland, Vt.: Charles E. Tuttle Co., 1957.

Serage, Nancy. *The Prince Who Gave Up A Throne: A Story of the Buddha.* New York: Thomas Y. Crowell, 1966.

Sohl, Robert, Carr, Audrey (Editors). *The Gospel According to Zen.* New York: Mentor, 1970.

Spiro, Melford E. *Buddhism and Society.* New York: Harper and Row, 1970.

Stryk, Lucien (Editor). *World of the Buddha.* Garden City, New York: Anchor Books, 1969.

Suzuki, Beatrice. *Mahayana Buddhism.* New York: MacMillan, (paperback) 1969.

Suzuki, D.T. *Manual of Zen Buddhism.* New York, Ballantine Books, 1974.

---*What is Zen?* New York: Harper and Row, 1972.

---*Zen Buddhism.* New York: Doubleday, 1949.

Watts, Alan. *This is It.* New York: Vintage Books, 1973.

---*The Spirit of Zen.* New York: Grove Press, 1958.

Yamada, S. *Brushwork of the Far East.* Rutland, Vt.: Japan Publications Trading Co., 1967.

B. **Audio Visuals:**

Filmstrips:

Haiku The Mood of Earth series. Laguna Beach, California: Lyceum Productions, Inc.

"Buddhism"–*Life Filmstrips.* New York, New York.

Films:

"Buddhism." Doubleday & Co., Inc., 501 Franklin Ave., Garden City, N.Y. 01531.

"The Buddha." Films, Inc., 1150 Wilmette Ave., Wilmette, Illinois 60091.

"The Buddhist World"–Coronet Films, 11 minutes. 65 E. S. Water St., Chicago, Illinois 60601.

C. **Addresses:** (for brochures, or booklets)

Buddhist Churches of America, Bureau of Buddhist Education, 1710 Octavia St., San Francisco, Calif.

or

Eastern Canada Buddhist Publications Toronto, Ontario, Canada

Confucianism, Taoism, and Shintoism

When Buddhism spread into China and Japan, it met three major indigenous religions growing up in those areas. In China, it met Confucianism and Toaism. In Japan, it met Shintoism. This chapter tells us about Confucianism, Taoism, and Shintoism. The two Chinese religions differ from each other, yet when put side by side they fill out a well-rounded view of life. Though we do not know to what extent these religions are practiced in China today, they are a part of the warp and woof of Chinese culture.

Confucianism

Confucianism began with the birth of K'ung-fu-tzu in 551 B.C. This sage, whose name was later Latinized into "Confucius," was a teacher *par excellence* who wished to be a government administrator. It was evident to Confucius that there was much need for reform in administrative offices, and he was a genius for this kind of reform. The problem was that no agency wanted to hire him because his impeccable honesty threatened some of the petty graft that was going on even in that ancient time.

When matters became too difficult, administrators in government would come to Confucius, in secret, for advice. But they feared to put him in charge. So most of the life of this humble teacher was spent with students. Today he is considered a teacher on a par with Socrates. Like Socrates he often taught while walking or riding with students, thus being a "parapatetic" teacher. Also, Confucius, like Socrates, had a way of drawing out answers which were already within his students. He taught by inquiry and discussion not by lecture and thus kept his students wrapt with interest. His students came from all walks of life – rich, poor, and in-between; yet he treated all as equals.

One legend states that, when Confucius was in his fifties, he was given a ruling position in his province of Lu. According to descriptions, the province became a model of perfection under his rule, so much so that valuables could be left by the roadsides and no one would take them. Honesty was the rule, and there was loyalty and good faith among all the citizens. But this kind of ideal rule did not last long, and soon Confucius was given a title that carried no power. Seeing the sham, he resigned and went back to teaching and advising.

After his death, his students collected his sayings, many of which were original and some of which Confucius had preserved from China's prior heritage. The *Sayings* of Confucius have been a source of etiquette, right action, and sound advice for all the centuries that have followed. A later follower, Mencius, expanded and elaborated upon Confucian precepts.

Today there are Confucian temples in China, and the birthday of Confucius is a national holiday in Taiwan, celebrated with dance and pageantry. Though the directives of Confucius seemed more ethical than religious, they have become the basis for a religion because Confucius felt that all his wisdom came from God. The honor and respect for ancestors in the Confucian tradition is expressed each year in family pilgrimages to graveyards where the tombs are decorated, and food and gifts are offered to the departed spirits.

The main thrust of the advice of Confucius is to make a concerted effort to get along in the cities with a maximum of harmony and accord. There are five precepts which Confucius left as guides for a harmonious kind of living:

1. **Jen.** *Jen* is the way of "human-heartedness" in which a person respects himself and respects his neighbor. "What you do not wish done to yourself, do not do to others," Confucius said in this respect. He also added the saying, "The man who possesses *jen*, wishing to establish himself, seeks also to establish others.

2. **Chun-tzu** This second quality for living is the name for a personal integrity which reflects itself in outward behavior. The person who knows his own worth does not have to boast, but quietly becomes poised, competent, and confident. He seeks more to serve than to be served.

3. **Li.** The third quality, *li*, has two meanings. It refers to *propriety* in honoring the name of the family and in respecting the elderly. It refers also to a *doctrine of the mean*, summed up in the saying "pleasure should not be carried to excess." The five relationships of *li* are summed up: "A ruler should be benevolent, a subject loyal; a father should be loving, a son reverential; an elder brother gentle, a younger brother respectful; a husband 'good,' a wife 'listening'; an elder friend considerate, a younger friend deferential."

4. **Te.** *Te* is the power necessary to rule, but it consists not of brute force but rather of moral example. The saying goes, "He who exercises government by means of his virtue may be compared to the north polar star which keeps its place and all the stars turn toward it."

5. **Wen.** The fifth precept according to Confucius is "the art of peace, in contrast to the art of war." It consists of the aesthetic arts: music, painting, poetry. Confucius believed that the nation with the highest culture is the nation which will ultimately triumph. No amount of power in the sense of force of arms will bring ultimate victory to a hollow or corrupt government.

Thus, by these directives for life Confucius exerted widespread and centuries-long influence upon his people. But contrast this polite man of the cities and towns to the next founder, whose domain is the rural areas, the mountains, hills, fields, and glades.

Taoism

The conscious effort of Confucius is in contrast to the relaxed, effortless strength of Lao Tzu. Lao Tzu, founder of Taoism, is said to have been born about 604 B.C. in a rural part of western China. So unpretentious was he, that the world today does not know even his real name. All that survives is the title given as "Lao Tzu" meaning "Grand Old Master."

According to the stories of his existence, this revered person was a "keeper of the archives" in his province, and exerted only a quiet influence among those who knew him. At the end of his life, as he was wandering to the western hills to spend his last days, the keeper of the Hankao Pass would not let him through until he had written down his wisdom for posterity. Stepping aside, Lao Tzu wrote down a book of poems which is entitled the *Tao Te Ching* (pronounced *Dow Day Jing*), meaning *The Way and its Power.* This short treatise, only 5,000 Chinese characters long, summarizes the rich resources for living that the "Old Master" had both collected and originated during his lifetime.

Having finished his written discourse, Lao Tzu mounted his water buffalo and passed on over into the western hills, never to be seen again. But the legacy he left behind has remained sacred scripture, and a guide to living for millions over all the ensuing centuries.

The message of the *Tao Te Ching* is that the "Way" is effortless and quiet, yet powerful. *Tao* means "Way," and it refers to a simple, quiet life style that has strength in its non-resistance. "The way to do is to be," goes the saying, and the being is in harmony with nature and all the universe. Tao is both a way and an essence – perhaps it could be defined as

"Ultimate Reality" or God. Like water, which seeks the lowest level, the Taoist seeks to blend his life in harmony with the elements in a "creative quietude" that is called *wu wei*. Not ruffled or flustered by events, not filled with anxiety or frantic effort, the Taoist lives in a serenity that is more than passive. For there is a strength to this living. Water seeking the lowest level also wears away the strongest granite over a period of time. Thus following the "Way," a Taoist is effective in his goals though passive in his actions. This principle is expressed poetically in the *Tao Te Ching*:

"The softest stuff in the world
Penetrates quickly the hardest;
Insubstantial, it enters
Where no room is.
By this I know the benefit
Of something done by quiet being;
In all the world, but few can know
Accomplishment apart from work,
Instruction where no words are used."
(Blakney, 1955, pg. 96)

The symbol of Taoism, called the *tai chi*, is a circle with one side dark and one side light. Yet in the dark side there is a spot of light and in the light side there is a spot of dark. This symbol shows that life is an interplay of opposites, and that there is a little of each in the other. What a contrast this concept is to the kind of television dramas that depict "good guys" and "bad guys" as if people could be completely one way or the other. The Taoist would be the first to recognize that there is a bit of each quality in the other.

Therefore Taoism advises "Never be too glad when you're glad, nor too sad when you're sad." For "He who feels punctured must have been a bubble." Not only is there some light in each darkness, but also it takes the full picture of light and darkness to make life in the full bloom of reality. It is a philosophy of life that does not ask "either – or" but affirms "both – and."

The dark side of the *tai chi* is called the *"yin"* and it represents such qualities as wet, dark, negative, soft, evil, cool, winter, and female. The light side, called the *"yang"* represents dry, light, positive, hard, good, warm, summer and male qualities. Though the listing of female with dark and negative qualities might sound male chauvinistic, the point is that all qualities are a part of a whole and all are essential.

The spirit of Taoism is well illustrated in one of the stories that comes out of China. The story is of a farmer whose only horse ran away. A neighbor came to console the farmer, but the only reply was, "Oh, who knows what is good or bad?" The next day, the horse returned, bringing with it a whole herd of wild horses. This time the neighbor came over to congratulate the farmer, but again the farmer replied, "Who knows what is good or bad?" On the third day, the farmer's son mounted one of the wild horses to break him, and in the process was himself thrown to the ground where he broke his leg. Upon hearing of the son's misfortune, the neighbor came to tell the farmer of his sorrow. But the farmer only replied, "Who knows what is good or bad?" On the fourth day, some government agents came to draft the farmer's son into the army, but seeing that he had a broken leg, they deferred him. The neighbor, hearing the news, came to tell of his gladness, but the farmer, in his infinite wisdom again replied, "Who knows what is good or bad?" The story goes on and on, emphasizing an effective resignation to *yin* and *yang*.

One of the greatest of Chinese Taoists, Chuang Tzu, told of a butcher whose knife did not get dull for twenty years. When questioned about how this could be, he answered simply: "Between the bones of every joint there is always some space, otherwise there could be no movement. By seeking out this space and passing through it my cleaver lays wide the bones without touching them." (Smith, 1958, pg. 205). The spaces of life, when utilized fully, can be as important as the substance. It has been said that the medical art of acupuncture naturally comes from Chinese culture because it, too, involves finding the open spaces for the easy insertion of the needles. Here is a poem from the *Tao Te Ching* expressing the value of pauses and open spaces in life:

Thirty spokes will converge
In the hub of a wheel;
But the use of the cart
Will depend on the part
Of the hub that is void.

With a wall all around
A clay bowl is molded;
But the use of the bowl
Will depend on the part
Of the bowl that is void.

Cut out windows and doors
In the house as you build
But the use of the house
Will depend on the space
Of the walls that is void.

So advantage is had
From whatever is there;
But usefulness rises
From whatever is not.
(Blakney, 1955, pg. 63)

Unfortunately, in popular practice, Taoism has become overlaid with superstition, so that Taoist priests go through elaborate rituals which resemble magic more than religion. The masses of Taoists are caught up with practices that are full of sorcery and necromancy, falling far short of the creative quietude of philosophic Taoism. Divination is popular in the form of fortune-telling through the casting of sticks. Yet for the more educated Chinese, the basic philosophy of Taoism and its poetry remain a major part of culture.

Closely akin to the philosophy of *tai chi* is the method of *I Ching* which consists of a systematic approach to analyzing the constant changes in life. *I Ching* is a system composed of the combination of broken *(yin)* and unbroken *(yang)* lines in sets of trigrams and hexagrams. In a series of sixty-four combinations, all facets of life are represented, and many Chinese Taoists use these combinations as guides in decision making.

Tai Chi Ch'uan

Taoism is expressed not only in the poetic words of Lao Tzu but also the graceful art of *Tai Chi Ch'uan*. This whole-self art consists of a systematic succession of body movements which expresses the quiet ease of the spirit of Taoism. The movements are made slowly, smoothly, and evenly, resembling the buoyancy of slow motion films. The arm motions are circular, sometimes making larger, sometimes making smaller circles. But the arms in *Tai Chi Ch'uan* are not posed at harsh angles. The use of the circular arm movements is to express the rounded symbol of the *tai chi*. Although this art resembles dance, it is not put to music and is not considered a dance form. It may also resemble calisthenics or exercise, and indeed it is considered excellent for physical conditioning. Yet *Tai Chi Ch'uan* is not mere gymnastics. In America, some have called the art "shadow boxing," since it is often practiced by partners mirroring each other's motions. Yet in the final analysis, it is not a sport. The only way to categorize *Tai Chi Ch'uan* is to put it in a descriptive category all to itself, to recognize its uniqueness, and to spread the news of this beneficial art form.

We in the Western Hemisphere, who often "knock ourselves out in the effort of trying," can learn something from the spirit of Taoism. The *wu wei*, the creative quietude, can be paraphrased in Western thought in the words, "Let go, let God." Not completely passive nor rampantly active, *wu wei* is the kind of blending with nature that characterizes an effective swimmer. He does not flounder or beat the elements but merges himself into the stream and works with the waters. *Wu wei* is also seen in the skillful wood carver who works with, not against, the grain of the wood.

In a sense, we could say that Confucianism and Taoism together make up the *"yin"* and *"yang"* of Chinese philosophy. The concerted effort of Confucianism, for a life of etiquette and effectiveness in the cities is one component, balanced by the effortless *"wu wei"* of Taoist "creative quietude." Perhaps there is a bit of one in the other, as in the completed circle of the *tai chi*. At any rate Confucianism and Taoism remain as the two indigenous religions of China, and together with Mahayana Buddhism they constitute the three religions which most Chinese embrace either separately or in a syncretic mix. Many Chinese temples find a place for all three.

Shintoism

Japan with its many religions has one main religion that grew up on its own soil. Shintoism is the one indigenous religion in Japan. It is practiced today as worshippers come a few at a time to quiet shrines nested in the hills and secluded spots of nature, or unobtrusively in towns and cities. But the Shinto shrine never calls attention to itself; rather it provides a place where worshippers can come as their need urges, to talk to the priest, to take measures to "ward off evil spirits" and to placate the "good spirits."

Originally, Shintoism was a polytheistic religion, as worshippers in ancient Japan prayed to the spirits of the sun, or the moon, or the wind. They tried to attract the help of good spirits while warding off the evil ones. Often today the worshippers at a Shinto shrine will place a paper on a pole or rope to detract evil from themselves. Yet the ancient beliefs in the "gods" are somewhat concentrated today in a more unified prayer to the "God of good spirits."

Ancient mythology explains the origin of Japan in this way: Long ago in the seventh generation of the gods, there lived two spirits, Izanagi and Izanami, who decided to descend from heaven to earth. They took a jeweled spear and pierced the sky which separated heaven from earth, until the spear touched the earthly waters. They stirred, and pulled back the spear. The foam on the spear dripped off to form the islands that are now Japan. Then they went down to live on these islands. Soon they gave birth to three "Noble Children," the Sun Goddess, the Moon God, and the Storm God. The Sun Goddess, *Amaterasu-Omi-Kami*, had a family, and her grandson Jimmu Tenno became the first emperor of Japan.

The emperors of Japan were thus considered divine, up until the end of World War II when Emperor Hirohito declared that he was human, not divine. But the religion did not die with his denouncement. Something of the ardent patriotism may have waned, but the religion took new turns. Though state Shinto was disestablished, cult Shinto remains, and the shrines rely on donations for support. Yet, they abound in many locations, and also sponsor festivals and parades at intervals during the year.

There are five major Shinto festivals in Japan: the New Year festival; the Girls' Festival (Peach Festival) on the third day of the third month; the Boys' Festival (Iris Festival) on the fifth day of the fifth month; the Summer Festival (of the Star Vega) on the seventh day of the seventh month; and the Indian Summer or Chrysanthemum Festival on the ninth day of the ninth month. In addition to these five specific festivals are others such as the Cherry Blossom Festival, the Emperor's Birthday celebration, and the First Fruits of Harvest Festival.

There are also the rites of the agricultural year such as when the seed is sewn, when the first blades appear, and when the tasting of the new rice is celebrated. Many Japanese are both Shinto and Buddhist, and celebrate Shinto festivals but request Buddhist funerals.

In each home of Japanese Shinto worshippers is the *kami-dana* or god shelf. On it are tablets with the name of an ancestor and of a patron deity of the home. There may also be a sacred mirror and strips of paper containing sacred texts. The families offer prayers and place offerings before the *kami-dana* each day. If there is a crisis in the families, the prayers are intensified and tapers are lit.

On the Girls' Day Festival, an array of dolls is arranged on shelves, with emperor and empress dolls on the highest shelf. On the Boys' Festival, a pole is placed before the home, with a colored "carp" banner for each boy in that house.

At the Shinto shrine, there are *torii*, gateway posts, consisting of two upright poles and two poles across the top, the upper one extending beyond the lower. Often there are several *torii* through which worshippers walk as they approach the shrine. The feeling is that as a worshipper walks under the *torii* on the way to the shrine he casts off all his cares and arrives ready to concentrate on the spirit of the religion.

Inside each shrine are sacred relics which nobody but the priest can see. It is felt that there is a sort of efficacy to having these relics, a power to ward off evil spirits and draw attention from the good spirits. Once a year the relics, still concealed in a case, are paraded through the town.

This writer once visited a Shinto shrine on a weekday morning to find a worshipper talking to the priest. They both sat crosslegged on the straw mat floor of the shrine, and they immediately invited their guest in to talk with them. The worshipper said earnestly, "You will never know how much it means to be able to come here and talk when there are worries. I go away refreshed having shared my burden." This new trend toward having priests as counselors in Shintoism is a new strength in an ancient religion. Though there are not regular services of worship, the shrines are always accessible, and they symbolize a life close to nature and earth. The very name Shinto reflects the word "Tao" that is found to mean "Way" in Taoism. Shin, meaning gods, gives a translation of the whole name as "Way of the gods."

Yin and Yang

Japan's Yasukuni Shrine at Tokyo. This Shinto shrine has long been considered the resting place of the souls of the nation's war dead.

Discussion Questions on Confucianism, Taoism, and Shintoism

1. In what way was Confucius an excellent teacher?
2. Why do you suppose that Confucius was not made ruler of all China?
3. In the long run, was he more influential as a teacher than as a ruler? Explain.
4. Contrast Lao-tzu with Confucius.
5. Can you think of a time in your life when you have taken a "Taoist" attitude toward some problem or worry? Describe this Taoist attitude.
6. Why does it take both *yin* and *yang* to complete the full circle of life? How does this view differ from an *either-or* view?
7. Do you think the Taoist would purposely cause evil to balance the good?
8. What is the value of empty spaces in Taoist thinking?
9. Explain *wu wei*.
10. Shinto mythology gives a poetic description of the origin of Japanese islands. Can you imagine from the story how the Japanese people feel about their homeland?

Bibliography on Confucianism, Taoism, and Shintoism

A. **Books:**

Primary Sources:

Blofield, John, *I Ching, The Book of Change*. New York: E.P. Dutton & Co., 1965.

Blakney, R.B. (Translator) *The Way of Life, Lao Tzu*. New York: New American Library, 1955.

Ware, James R. (Translator) *The Sayings of Confucius*. New York: New American Library, 1955.

Secondary Sources:

Delza, Sophia. *Tai Chi Ch'uan*. N. Canton, Ohio: Good News Publishing Co., 1961.

Fingarette, Herbert, *Confucius–The Secular as Sacred*. New York: Harper Torch Books, 1972.

Holtom, D.C. *Modern Japan and Shinto Nationalism*. Chicago: University Press.

Liu, Da. *Tai Chi Ch'uan and I Ching*. New York: Harper and Row, 1972.

Maisel, Edward. *Tai Chi for Health*. New York: Holt, Rinehart, and Winston, 1963.

Soong, Mayting. *The Art of Chinese Paper Folding for Young and Old*. New York: Harcourt, Brace, 1948.

B. **Audio-Visuals:**

Records:

"China's Instrumental Heritage," Lyrichord Discs, Inc., 141 Perry St., New York, N.Y.

"World Library of Folk and Primitive Music," Alan Lomax–Columbia Masterworks, Japan; the Ryukyus, Formosa.

Filmstrips:

"Families of the World" Series, *China.*

"China and Her Neighbors" Series, *China, Past and Present.*

"Children of the Orient" Series, *Ming Li of China.*

(All three of the above are available from McGraw-Hill, Text Film Division, 330 W. 42nd St., New York, N.Y. 10036.

"The World's Great Religions" Series, *Confucianism and Taoism*, available from Time-Life.

Films:

"Chinese Shadow Play"–Contemporary Films, Inc., 828 Custer Ave., Evansville, Ill. 60602.

"The Ancient Orient: The Far East"

"The Golden Rule: A Lesson for Beginners"

(Both of the above are available from Coronet Films, 65 East S. Water St., Chicago, Ill. 60601.

Judaism

The scene shifts now from the "Far East" to the "Near East," and we note that about 4000 years ago while the bards sang their chants along the Indus River in India, the family of Abraham began the migration from Ur to Haran and down into Cannaan, which is today the State of Israel. Out of the wanderings of these ancient peoples, later known as the Hebrews, has come the religious tradition that shapes Western thought to a remarkable degree.

Later writers in the Hebrew tradition reflected on their history from the days of Abraham and down through the Exodus from Egypt in these words:

> "A wandering Aramaean was my father; and he went down into Egypt and sojourned there, few in number; and there he became a nation, great, mighty, and populous. And the Egyptians treated us harshly, and afflicted us, and laid upon us hard bondage. Then we cried to the Lord the God of our father, and the Lord heard our voice, and saw our affliction, our toil, and our oppression; and the Lord brought us out of Egypt with a mighty hand and an outstretched arm, with great terror, with signs and wonders; and he brought us into this place and gave us this land, a land flowing with milk and honey."
>
> (Deuteronomy 26:5-9)

It is this dual affirmation of Judaism – that God is personal, and that He cares actively for His people–which has made this religion powerful in its own right and also a basis from which other Western religions have grown.

Historians have never ceased to marvel that the Hebrews, later known as the Jews, have wielded such positive influence in spite of the hardships they have suffered, century after century. Over six million Jews were put to death by the Nazis in this century. Though few in number–about fourteen million in all today–and scattered over the face of the globe, the Jews have a sense of common destiny and purpose, guided by a sense of "Presence," unsurpassed in all of history. The state of Israel is of particular importance as a homeland for those who live elsewhere.

Modern Jewish Theology

Although Judaism is a religion deeply rooted in history, it is also a way of life for its millions of followers. With its strong emphasis on improving the quality of daily living, it stands in contrast to the elements in other religions which stress the importance of escape from life. Judaism, in the words of one of its recent theologians Dr. Martin Buber, is a call for the "hallowing of this life." In his book *I and Thou*, Dr. Buber goes on to say that religion should not be a matter of detachment from life, but rather such full and responsible living that, " . . . if you hallow this life, you meet the living God." (Pg. 79)

The quality of religious living, according to Dr. Buber, is summed up in the primary wording "*I-Thou.*" This phrase describes the kind of relationship of concern in which two people care about one another with no ulterior motive – each cares for the sake of the other. Such a genuine concern, then, becomes not just a human dimension but a "triatic" relationship as, " . . . the extended lines of relations meet in the eternal Thou." (Pg. 75)

Another modern Jewish theologian, Dr. Abraham Joshua Heschel, states that man can behold God in his world basically in three ways: in nature, in history, and in the "sacred deed." First, in nature, Dr. Heschel says that man can become aware of God because His handiwork is spread through the fields, forests, mountains, and seas. A man stands in the woodlands watching a flood of sunlight scatter through the open spaces between the leaves and branches. He is caught up by the sense of awe and wonder engendered by the grandeur around him. His inward response is reflected in the words of the prophet Isaiah, "Holy, holy, holy is the Lord of hosts; the whole earth is full of His glory." (Isaiah 6:3) This response in faith is the Jewish affirmation that all of life is sanctified, and that man beholds the Creator by looking at His creation. In fact, there is a special Hebrew phrase appropriate to new life which many Jews still say to new parents: "May you raise your child to a life blessed with Torah, marriage and good deeds." The phrase is contained in the ritual observance marking a Jewish infant's entry into the world.

When Dr. Heschel states that man beholds God through nature, he is not saying that God and nature are one. Clearly he distinguishes between God and His handiwork. Man discerns what God is like by seeing what He has produced, according to Heschel, but through it all, there remains the mystery whereby God is both partly revealed and partly concealed. It is as if nature is the element of the sublime which points beyond itself. As Heschel states in *Between God and Man*,

> "The sublime, furthermore, is not necessarily related to the vast and overwhelming in size. It may be sensed in every grain of sand, in every drop of water. Every flower in the summer, every snowflake in the winter, may arouse in us the sense of wonder that is our response to the sublime." (Pg. 38)

This type of theology is not pantheism (such as one would find in Hinduism, for instance) but panentheism in which "God is clothed in His world, but remains separate." According to Heschel, every leaf on every tree is a letter from God. The truly religious response is "radical amazement." According to Dr. Heschel, "the earth is crammed with marvel" and man is thereby made aware of how marvelous is its Creator!

The second way God is revealed, according to Heschel, is through history. Biblical history is filled with events which the

Hebrews sensed to be acts of God.

By comparing the drama of human history to a tapestry with both horizontal and vertical threads, Heschel distinguishes between two kinds of happenings: processes and events. A process, he states, is a regular happening that follows a pattern or law such as night and day or the seasons. It is like a horizontal thread. It is predictable, happens in time and space, and can be described by the scientist. An event, on the other hand, is an unpredictable happening, with a transcendental dimension beyond time and space. It is like a vertical thread on the tapestry. The first event (vertical) was creation, which began the processes (horizontal) that now go on regularly. But the Jewish theistic attitude toward life affirms that God's care did not end with creation but rather continues through human history, manifested in events such as the call of Abraham and the subsequent narratives of Isaac, Jacob, and Joseph. Throughout these accounts, there is the sensitivity to God's presence, working through the lives of His people. The freeing of the Hebrew slaves in Egypt, through the instrumentality of Moses is the supreme example of God's saving action–the supreme event.

Another remarkable event in Jewish history is the return to Jerusalem after the Babylonian captivity. The voices of prophets such as Amos and Jeremiah are also a part of the vertical events. Thus, the Creator did not spawn the creation and step back from it. but continues to care and to intervene in events of history to alleviate the sufferings of men. Man senses such events not scientifically but poetically, as a metaphor speaks of a greater truth beyond.

The third way God is revealed in His world is through the sacred deeds of men. Deeds are called sacred not because of a connection with formal worship but because of their expression of concern, in the way that God has historically expressed His concern according to the beliefs of Judaism. Heschel describes two basic types of concern: *transitive* concern for others and *reflexive* concern for the self. Heschel goes on to point out that

God, Who need not be concerned for His own survival, can afford to be pure transitive concern. Animals are usually pure reflexive concern, taking care only of their own survival. Man, halfway between, has to have a certain amount of reflexive concern in order to protect himself. But to the extent that man goes on to show transitive concern for others is the extent to which he lives up to the image of God within himself. Thus, the deed that is called sacred is the *Mitzvah*, the deed of kindness for any neighbor. Man actually needs to be needed, and as he expresses his concern he expresses the religious dimension of his existence, according to the underlying theology of Judaism.

Thus, in the writings of Abraham Joshua Heschel, we have seen how God is revealed in nature, in history, and in the sacred deed. Heschel also goes on to show how men can experience holiness in time by celebrating the Jewish special days of religious observance. He calls the Sabbath a "sanctuary in time", an intersection of time and eternity. It is "the armistice in man's cruel struggle for existence, a truce in all conflicts, personal and social, . . . the exodus from tension, the liberation of man from his own muddiness . . . . " (1959 pg. 222) Let us therefore go on to learn of the meaning of the holy days of Judaism, beginning with the seventh day observance of *Shabbat* or Sabbath.

The Sabbath

The sabbath or *Shabbat* is the holy day that recurs every week in Judaism, always on the seventh day which begins at sundown on Friday and lasts until nightfall on Saturday. It is celebrated in Jewish homes, and also in the temples and synagogues, but always with the objective of rest, inner peace, and elevated spirits. It is biblically ordained in the creation account of Genesis where God is described as creating the world in six days and resting on the seventh; and in the Ten Commandments it is listed as fourth:

> "Remember the Sabbath day, to keep it holy. Six days you shall labor and do all your work; but the seventh day is a Sabbath to the Lord your God; in it you shall not do any work . . . ." (Exodus 20:8, 9)

The author Herman Wouk, in a book called *This is My God*, describes how the Sabbath feels in the life of a Jewish person. He tells of leaving the rush of work, while one of his plays is under production, and arriving home in time for the Sabbath:

> "My wife and boys, whose existence I have almost forgotten . . . are waiting for me, dressed in holiday clothes, and looking to me marvelously attractive. We have sat down to a splendid dinner, at a table graced with flowers and the old Sabbath symbols: the burning candles, the twisted loaves, the stuffed fish, and my grandfather's silver goblet brimming with wine. I have blessed my boys with the ancient blessing; we have sung the pleasantly syncopated Sabbath table hymns." (Pg. 39)

He goes on to say that the Sabbath is a day when his children know he will be home and he is not pressured by the ringing of the phone or the demands of the workaday world. But there is more to the Sabbath than the negation of pressure. There is also a positive quality of the Sabbath which Jews call *menuhah*. This is a term for "tranquility, serenity, peace, and repose." It is an inner calm, a foretaste of eternal life.

The Sabbath is ended in the home as the sundown approaches, and the *Havdalah* candle is lit to commemorate the close of the hallowed time. Sweet spices are smelled as a final memento to remind the families that at the end of six more days another Sabbath will be celebrated. There is a certain sadness at the close of the Sabbath, yet a renewed spirit and readiness for the week to come.

There are three branches of Judaism, and Sabbath services differ among the three. Reform, and some Conservative Jews go to the synagogue after the Friday evening Sabbath meal, but in other Conservative and in Orthodox families, the father goes to the synagogue before the meal. The main service at the synagogue for them is on Saturday morning. Many Conservative and Orthodox Jews also attend another service on Saturday afternoon. Their services have a high content of Hebrew language. Only Reform Jews have an organ and choir for their services, but Conservative Jews as well as Reform Jews allow men and women to sit together in the worship. The sermon and many prayers are in English in Reform and Conservative congregations. Orthodox and Conservative services are as close as possible to the ancient patterns of worship.

On the door of each Jewish home is a *mezuzah*, a small box containing 15 verses of the Torah. Each member of the family looks at or touches the *mezuzah* as he leaves home or returns. The words in the *mezuzah* reflect the main tenet of Judaism, the Shema: "Hear, O Israel, the Lord our God, the Lord is one," a prayer from the Book of Deuteronomy 6:4.

Other Holy Days

It is the first day of the Jewish month of Tishri (September or October on the secular calendar). Traditionally, this day has been set aside in Judaism as the celebration of Rosh Hashana , the beginning of a new year. The commandment to observe this day is found in the Bible in Leviticus 23:24, and the summons is for each worshipper to attend the synagogue assembly for prayer and self-examination. The climax of the solemn Rosh Hashana assembly is the blowing of the ram's horn, or *shofar*, to rouse man from moral laziness and bring him to a renewed awareness of his duties to other men and to God.

In Jewish homes, Rosh Hashana is observed by the dipping of bread or apples or figs into honey to symbolize the hope that sweetness will prevail in the coming year. Actually, Rosh Hashana is the beginning not only of a new year but of ten special days, "The Days of Awe," in which Jews search their souls for ways in which they can live better lives. For

Conservative and Orthodox Jews, two days of worship are set aside for Rosh Hashana , whereas Reform Jews observe Rosh Hashana on only one day.

The Yom Kippur fast is observed on the tenth day of "The Days of Awe," most special of all days. Jewish people flock to the synagogues and temples for the lengthy services which lead the people to a sense of repentance for all evils they may have done or good they may have neglected to do. During the twenty-five hour fast for this Day of Atonement, Jews must not eat, drink, engage in sexual activity, bathe, anoint the body, or wear leather shoes. The institution of this day is found in the Book of Leviticus, chapter 23, verses 26 - 31, and many embellishments have been added to the original command.

The confessions of the people on Yom Kippur are corporate – said as a body rather than individually. This corporate aspect of worship symbolizes the sense of belonging that unites all of Judaism.

Herman Wouk, in *This Is My God*, says of Yom Kippur observance:

> " The Hebrew People draws its optimism from its idea of the universe. Disaster, protracted poverty, mass murder, have never dissuaded the Jews from the vision caught at Mt. Sinai of an unseen God. They believe not only that he exists, but that he is interested in men; that he wants them to become better than they are; and that he gave them a law that points the way to a better world. . . . Perhaps the American Jew shows an old race wisdom in clinging to the High Holy Days, no matter how this hold slips for the moment in the rest of Judaism. The spirit of Yom Kippur is a spore out of which the structure of our old religion can grow again; for it is the germ of the whole, and it does not die." (Pg. 69)

Five days after Yom Kippur, the Festival of the Tabernacles, Succot, begins. This is an autumnal harvest thanksgiving observance, and it also commemorates the granting of food to Moses and his followers during their days in the wilderness. The week-long festival is celebrated especially on its first two and last two days. To observe this occasion, Jews build "tabernacles" or booths in which the families are to dine for the week. The booths (succot) are decorated in harvest fruits, in biblical times with four special branches across the top: branches of palm, ethrog, willow, and myrtle. Today , any covering such as grass, straw, or pine branches may be used. The traditional palm, ethrog, willow, and myrtle are used in a separate ritual for the holiday., The top of the booth must leave open spaces so that the families can gaze at the heavens. During the dinner there are psalms of praise, songs, and chants. This is a festive time of thanksgiving and special rejoicing. Though celebrated primarily in the homes, it is also celebrated in the synagogues with the waving of the branches and the "Hosannah" procession led by the cantor carrying the scrolls of the Torah. "Hosannah" means "(Lord) please save." Leviticus 23: 33-44 describes the ordinance for this Feast of Booths.

At the end of Succot, there is a celebration called Simhat Torah which means "Rejoicing in the Torah." This event commemorates the ending of the reading of the Torah for that year, and the beginning again for the new year. The Torah (five books from Genesis through Deuteronomy) is divided so that the readings are completed in one year of study. The word Torah is best translated as "teaching" or "instruction." Parades and excitement with music and joy fill the synagogue as the congregation marches seven times around, carrying the sacred scrolls of the Torah. Herman Wouk remembers:

> "My grandfather, patriarchal and reserved all year long, was still performing this dance in his nineties, a few shuffling, tottering steps, his face alight with pleasure as he clasped the Torah in his old arms." (1973 pg. 57)

A worshipper, called the Bridegroom of the Torah, reads the last lines of the Book of Deuteronomy, and the next reader, called Bridegroom of Genesis, begins anew the reading of the Torah with the words, "In the beginning . . . " as jubilation fills the house of worship.

The next celebration in the Jewish calendar year is the Festival of Hanukkah. This comes sometime around the month of December on the secular calendar, but precisely on the twenty-fifth of Kislev on the Jewish calendar . It commemorates the time about 160 B.C. when the Jews had been overcome by the Syrians and were asked to worship idols instead of their own God. The Jewish temple in Jerusalem was desecrated, and those who refused to bow before the Syrian gods were killed. Finally, outraged by the suffering, a leader, Matthias, and his sons rose up to lead the Jews in a freedom struggle which culminated in the defeat of the Syrians. Matthias and his sons are called "Maccabees" which means, "hammers". The Jews immediately set about restoring worship in their temple. But they found that there was only enough oil in the eternal light to burn one day. It took eight days to make ritually pure oil. Yet by an unknown blessing, which Jews have henceforth called a miracle, the oil burned for the full eight days, signifying to them that God's presence is always with them. Hanukkah commemorates the miracle of the oil.

To celebrate Hanukkah, Jews have a special *menorah*, or candle holder, that holds eight candles plus a lighter candle called a *shamash*. With the *shamash*, they light one candle on the first night of the Hanukkah Festival of Lights. They light two candles on the second night, three on the third, and so on until, on the eighth night all eight candles are glowing. During the burning of the candles (about a half hour) no work is done, and families enjoy being together with games and music. Traditional refreshments for the celebration are *latkes* (potato pancakes) or doughnuts (in Jerulalem) and nuts and candies. In America presents are often exchanged during the eight days but traditionally small amounts of money were given to youngsters once during the holiday. The dreydel game, which originated for Hanukkah celebration several centuries ago in Germany, is described in the Learning Activities section following this chapter.

On the fourteenth of Adar, usually in February or March, Purim is celebrated with the reading of the Book of Esther. After the evening prayers in the synagogue, the reading of the book begins. But the solemnity of the occasion is soon interrupted as the audience (abounding in children) makes loud noises to hiss the villain, Haman, and to cheer the hero, Mordecai, and heroine, Esther. The next day there is much more merriment as the story is acted in melodrama fashion, and there are feasts and the giving of food to the poor.

One of the most important holy occasions of the year is the celebration of Passover, which comes in March or April. This observance commemorates the time when the Hebrews were slaves in Egypt and were spared from the plagues which struck Egypt before their Exodus to freedom. The Passover is celebrated with particular significance in Jewish homes. A best tablecloth is used, and spread with special dishes. Because their forefathers left Egypt in haste, not waiting for the yeast in the bread to rise, Jews use special unleavened bread, called *matzo* for Passover.

Before Passover, the Jewish housewife cleans the house to be certain that it is free from all unleavened bread. The children help in the search, and it becomes almost like a game to see who can do most to get rid of the leavened bread. There is a special order to the *Seder* (ritual order) of Passover. The foods for the *Seder* dinner are special and the ritual retells the story of the Exodus in an unforgettable way. The smallest child asks four traditional questions from the *Hagadah* or order of service, and as the father answers them, the story of the Exodus unfolds. The full observance of Passover lasts a week, and Reform Jews hold special celebrations on just the first and last days. Conservative and Orthodox Jews celebrate Passover for eight days with special celebrations on the first two and last two days.

Passover also commemorates the earth's awakening fertility. In olden days, an omer of barley was brought to the Temple on the second day of Passover. Seven weeks or 50 days later, the harvest of the first fruits is celebrated by Shavuot or Pentecost. Shavuot means "weeks" in Hebrew; Pentecost means "fiftieth day" in Greek. It also and more significantly commemorates the giving of the Law to Moses, which took place 50 days after the Passover. Thus, Shavuot is both a nature festival and an historic celebration. The festival of Shavuot today is celebrated in synagogues and homes by decorations of flowers and branches, and the serving of special dairy foods at the main festive meal. The story of Ruth is read from the Bible.

What we see most clearly from this recounting of Jewish holy days is the flair of this culture for dramatic re-enactment of history and the cycles of nature; for the providence of God is seen in both nature and history and the many celebrations serve to keep the people ever mindful.

The Messianic Era

In the past, all Jews looked forward to the coming of the Messiah, a servant of God who would bring lasting peace and plenty to the earth. Today, many still await a personal Messiah, and others look forward to an age of peace which they call the Messianic Era. Those espousing this second interpretation consider themselves responsible in helping to bring this peace about, but await the Era as coming through the instrumentality of many persons rather than one.

Whether it is one or many who will usher in the Messianic Era, it is the fulfillment of ancient predictions that this Era will come about through the actions of the descendants of Abraham. The promise to Abraham in Genesis 12:3 states, "I will bless them that bless you, and him who curses you I will curse, and by you all the families of the earth will be blessed." Thus, it is both divine initiative and human faithfulness that is to be the source of redemption of mankind. This great Hebrew tradition asserts that the eventual salvation of the world will come when all men reject idolatry and accept one God and that the Messianic Era will be the Kingdom of God.

Jewish pilgrims flock to the Wailing Wall in Jerusalem.

Blowing the shofar. Note the Torah and other symbolism in background, and prayer shawl (tallit) and skullcap (yarmulka).

Young people take part in a traditional Jewish folk dance.

Discussion Questions on Judaism

1. What does the Jewish author, Dr. Martin Buber, mean by the term *"I-thou"*? Are there people in your life with whom you feel a real *"I-thou"* relationship? Describe.
2. In Buber's theology, what *three* persons or entities are present in a true *"I-thou"* encounter?
3. In what three ways does Dr. Heschel believe God can be known in His world?
4. From the ideas of Dr. Buber and Dr. Heschel, would you feel that Judaism is more a religion of this life or of a life after death? Explain.
5. What is the supreme Event in Jewish history? Can you tell about it in your own words? Would you describe it differently if you were a newspaper reporter, than if you were one of the liberated Hebrews? Would both accounts be valid?
6. How is the Exodus re-lived in the Passover Seder?
7. How do you explain the fact that the Jews, the smallest number of persons among major world religions, scattered over the face of the globe and persecuted century after century, have maintained a sense of identity and purpose and a consistent set of values?
8. What is the Torah, and why is it so important in Judaism?
9. Describe the Jewish celebration of the Festival of Succot. What customs are observed? What meaning is transmitted by the celebration?
10. What is meant by the Messianic Era? Is there more than one interpretation?

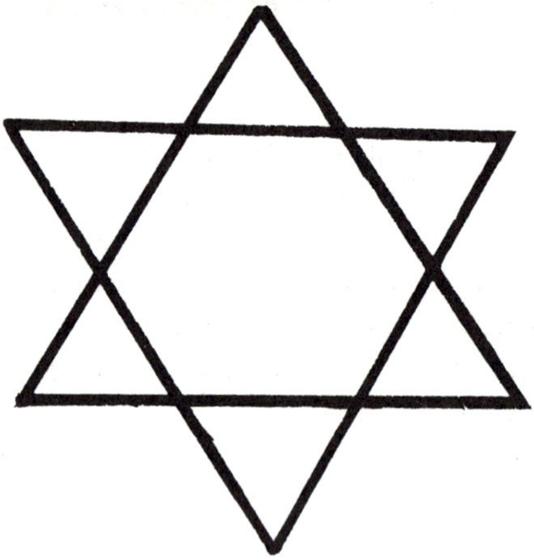

Star of David
symbol of Judaism

Bibliography on Judaism

A. **Books**

Primary sources:

The Hebrew Bible

The Torah

The Talmud

Secondary Sources:

Adler, Morris, *The World of the Talmud.* New York: Schocken Books, 1963.

Buber, Martin, *I and Thou.* New York: Charles Scribner's Sons, 1923.

–––*Between Man and Man.* London: Keegan-Paul, 1947.

–––*Israel and the World.* New York: Schocken Books, 1948.

Cronback, Abraham, *Judaism for Today.* New York: Bookman Assn. 1954.

Dimont, Max, *Jews, God, and History.* New York: Simon and Schuster, 1962.

Gilbert, Arthur, *Your Neighbor Celebrates.* New York: Friendly House, 1957.

Heschel, Abraham J., *Between God and Man.* New York: The Free Press, 1959.

–––*Man's Quest for God.* New York: Charles Scribner's Sons, 1954.

–––*Israel (An echo of eternity).* New York: Farrar, Straus and Giroux, 1969.

Image of the Jews, Teachers' Guide to Jews and their Religion. New York: Anti-Defamation League of B'nai B'rith, 1970.

Kertzer, Morris. *What is a Jew?* New York: The MacMillan Co., 1965.

Margolis, I. and Markowitz, S. *Jewish Holidays and Festivals*. New York: The Citadel Press, 1962.

Scharfstein, Sol, *Draydel, Draydel, Draydel*. New York: Ktav Publishing House, 1969.

Sol, Robert, *The First Book of Chanukah*. New York: Ktav Publishing House, 1956.

Steinberg, Milton, *Basic Judaism*. New York: Harcourt, Brace and World, 1947.

Wouk, Herman, *This is My God*. New York: Pocket Books, 1973.

Zborowski, M. *Life is with People*. New York: Schocken Books, 1952.

For an excellent and comprehensive list of books, pamphlets, and audio-visual materials, write for the catalog *Teaching About Jews and Judaism*, available without charge from Anti-Defamation League of B'nai B'rith, 315 Lexington Ave., New York, N.Y. 10016.

B. Audio-Visuals

Records:

"Hanukkah, The Feast of Lights," Sung by Emanuel Rosenberg. New York, Ktav Publications (records for other Jewish holidays also available here)

"Hanukkah at Home"—National Women's League of the United Synagogue of America (Conservative)

"Hebrew Religious Chants" by Rabbi Hyman Millman, Everest Records, 10920 Wilshire Blvd., Suite 410, Los Angeles, Calif. 90024.

"Music of a People"—Stanley Black conducting the London Festival Orchestra and Chorus

The Jewish Kit (items used in worship from B'nai B'rith Anti-Defamation League, 315 Lexington Ave., New York, New York.)

Filmstrips:

"The World's Great Religions," *Judaism*, Time-Life.

"Families Around the World" Series. *Family of Israel.*

"Great Stories from the Old Testament" Series.

Both of the above available from Encyclopedia Britannica, 425 N. Michigan Ave., Chicago, Ill. 60611.

"The World Believes" Series. *Judaism Today*, Society for Visual Education, 1345 Diversey Parkway, Chicago, Ill. 60614.

"Abraham," "Jacob," "Joseph," "Moses," "Amos," "Nehemiah," "Passover,"–United Church Press, 1505 Race St., Philadelphia, Pa. 19102.

JESUS

Christianity

Christianity grew out of Judaism with the emergence of the historic figure of Jesus of Nazareth who came to be called the Christ. The title, "Christ" literally means "anointed." Anointing in the ancient world was symbolic of recognizing the role of kingship or great leadership. It designated a chosen-ness, a special realization of worth.

To the historian, Jesus of Nazareth was a Jewish carpenter's son who grew up in the town of Nazareth not far from the Sea of Galilee. His life span was about 33 years, and most that is known of him is concentrated into the last three years of his life. Gathering a small band of disciples around him, he traveled the length and breadth of Palestine, befriending the friendless, healing the sick or making broken persons whole, and proclaiming the immanence of the Kingdom of God's love. Roman authorities feared his popularity with the masses of people. Zealots who thought he would lead a revolution against the oppressive Roman rule of that day were disappointed with him. Traditionalists looked askance at his fresh interpretation of scriptures. In the final week of his life, Jesus was brought to trial and eventually put to death at the hands of Roman officials, by means of crucifixion.

Yet the end was really the beginning of a new era. Those who had been close to Jesus in his lifetime believed his spirit still with them by means of an event which they termed the Resurrection. The impact of the event was so moving that followers risked their lives, often enduring persecution and torture, to proclaim the message of Jesus whom they had come to believe was "truly the Son of God." The followers of Jesus, who first called themselves followers of "the Way," began traveling far and wide to proclaim his message of God's love for all people, and began gathering small bands of persons into organizations later known as churches.

History became divided into a new era in which time is reckoned from the beginning of Jesus' life. Today, there are over one billion followers of Jesus, called Christians. Christianity is the most widespread of all religions, and claims the largest number of adherents. There are those who lament the fact that not all who claim the title of Christian live up to all the precepts of the religion. Yet from the outstanding ones who have lived up to the Christ-like life style, we can glimpse something of the meaning and message of Christianity. Let us begin with a Japanese Christian.

Toyohiko Kagawa

Toyohiko Kagawa was born in Kobe, Japan, in 1888. During his youth, he met and was influenced by Christian missionaries and he enrolled at Meiji Christian College in Tokyo and later at Kobe Seminary. When he was 21, Kagawa was so overcome by the feeling of warmth and love that he had found in Christianity that he was determined to leave his comfortable home and spend his life in the slum areas of his city, ministering to the people who needed him most. His Buddhist family disowned him for such a decision but loading his few possessions, mostly books, onto a wheelbarrow, Kagawa moved into the heart of the city. There he rented a room that was scarcely larger than a closet, and cost only five cents a day. The reason this room was so inexpensive was that previously a man had been murdered there and the stain of his blood was still on the floor. Others feared that the ghost of the slain man would come back to haunt the room, but Kagawa had no such fear.

Immediately Kagawa began befriending the friendless in the way that he felt Jesus had done. He ate with the outcast and visited the sick. Once a man in a drunken rage came to Kagawa's door, brandishing a sharp sword and determined to plunge it into someone's heart. Kagawa bowed in prayer, then entered into conversation with the man, who departed, leaving his sword as a gift.

Soon the very presence of Kagawa in the area became a leavening influence. Persons in need came to him, and he helped in whatever way he could. Often, however, it was very frustrating to Kagawa to realize how limited his help had to be. In a book he wrote, called *Songs from the Slums*, he lamented his inability to help as much as he would have liked:

"Penniless

Penniless . . .
A while
Without food
I can live;
But it breaks my heart
To know
I cannot give.

Penniless . . .
I can share my rags,
But I –
Cannot bear to hear
Starved children cry.

Penniless . . .
And rain falls,
But trust is true.
Helpless, I wait to see
What God will do."

(pg. 70)

Out of the frustrations of trying to help persons one at a time, Kagawa began to feel God's call for him to serve in a way in which he could help on a larger scale. In order to know how to do this effectively, he came to America in 1914, stayed through 1916 and studied at Princeton University. Then he returned to Japan to work with such helpful groups as Mission to Lepers, International Peace Association, Moral New Life Society, Medical Co-operative, Credit Co-operative, and Tree Crop Agricultural Research Institute. He also organized churches, kindergartens, and nurseries.

Kagawa served as pastor of one of the churches in Kobe. He also addressed groups of people wherever he found them – in the park or on street corners. Once, in the middle of his Sunday sermon, Kagawa was given a message that two opposing groups were about to converge in a street fight. Closing his service quickly, he hopped into a rickshaw and asked the driver to take him to the street corner where the fight was imminent. Kagawa spoke no word to the two groups, but merely stood at the intersection of the two streets so that they would have to push him aside when they clashed. His presence as a man of peace was so well established by that time, that the two groups turned and went their respective ways unharmed by each other.

In 1939, Kagawa spoke out against the militarism of his own government. Considering him a disloyal citizen, the government imprisoned Kagawa. He was forced to wear a threadbare kimono and to live in a prison cell that was literally swarming with mosquitoes. He told of having to cover himself, head and all, with the kimono, leaving only enough room for his nose to breathe. Yet in spite of these miserable circumstances, he managed to spend his prison days constructively by meditating and by writing poems on his longing to help others as Jesus did. One verse he penned sums up his aspirations. It is called "Discovery":

"I cannot invent
New Things,
Like the airships
Which sail
On silver wings;
But today

A wonderful thought
In the dawn was given,
And the stripes on my robe,
Shining from wear,
Were suddenly fair,
Bright with light
Falling from heaven –
Gold, and silver, and bronze
Lights from the windows of heaven.

And the thought
Was this:
That a secret plan
Is hid in my hand;
That my hand is big,
Big,
Because of that plan.

That God,
Who dwells in my hand,
Knows this secret plan
Of the things he will do for the world
Using my hand!"
(pp. 66-67)

When Toyohiko Kagawa was finally released from prison, he directed a number of social service agencies in Japan. His "hand" was used for easing much human suffering in the world, just as he had envisioned! His work on behalf of the poor and the sick was patterned after the words and deeds of Jesus.

Martin Luther King, Jr.

Freedom for oppressed people was the cause for which the Reverend Dr. Martin Luther King, Jr. gave his life. As pastor of Dexter Avenue Baptist Church in Montgomery, Alabama, this

Negro nonviolent fighter for civil rights led one struggle after another, beginning with the now famous bus boycott of 1956. This boycott was caused by an age-old ruling that "colored persons" had to go to the back of any public bus, even if it meant standing up while there were vacant seats in the front of the bus. After valiant efforts, the cause was won, but not without hardship and terror. And after the victory, there still remained many other injustices to be overcome. In spite of the fact that he was imprisoned, fined, insulted, wounded, and bombed, Dr. King continued relentlessly to work for the civil rights of his people.

Born in Atlanta, Georgia, in 1929, son and grandson of ministers, Martin Luther King, Jr. advanced so rapidly in school that he was permitted to enter college at the age of fifteen. From college, he entered Crozier Theological Seminary where he was president of the student body and graduated with the highest record in his class. This high academic achievement won him the opportunity to go on to Boston University for his degree of Ph.D. Among the many books which Dr. King studied were the writings of India's great Mahatma Gandhi, leader of the world's first nonviolent revolution. Dr. King later stated that the actions he took in winning civil rights were "grounded in the spirit of Jesus and the techniques of Gandhi."

After the Montgomery episode, there were many more marches, "sit-ins," and other demonstrations which Dr. King led for social justice. The effort was not without a heavy price of suffering. Dr. King and many of his people were reviled and affronted, but their response was "We have come to the point where we are able to say to those who will even use violence to block us, we will match your capacity to inflict suffering with our capacity to endure suffering." (Time-Life, 1968, pg. 18) Men, women, and children lost their lives in the freedom effort, but the work continued, guided by Dr. King's Southern Christian Leadership Conference.

In the spring of 1963, plans got underway for a march on Washington which culminated with 200,000 persons – black and white together – moving in unison from the Washington Monument to the Lincoln Memorial. There, on the front steps, Dr. King gave his famous "I Have a Dream" speech which said, in part:

> "I have a dream that one day this nation will rise up, live out the true meaning of its creed: 'We hold these truths to be self-evident that all men are created equal.'
>
> I have a dream that one day on the red hills of Georgia sons of former slaves and the sons of former slave-owners will be able to sit down together at the table of brotherhood. I have a dream that one day even the state of Mississippi, a state sweltering with the heat of injustice, sweltering with the heat of oppression, will be transformed into an oasis of freedom and justice.
>
> I have a dream that my four little children will one day live in a nation where they will not be judged by the color of their skin but by the content of their character.
>
> I have a dream that one day every valley shall be exalted, every hill and mountain shall be made low. The rough places will be made plain, and the crooked places will be made straight. This is the faith that I go back to the south with . . . .
>
> When we allow freedom to ring – when we let it ring from every city and every hamlet, from every state and every city, we will be able to speed up that day when all God's children, black men and white men, Jews and Gentiles, Protestants and Catholics, will be able to join hands and sing in the words of the Negro Spiritual, 'Free at last, Free at last, Great God a-mighty. We are free at last!'"
>
> (Time-Life, 1968, pg. 57)

In 1964, the Civil Rights Act was passed making discrimination in many places illegal. But there was still much work to be done. When Martin Luther King, Jr. was awarded the Nobel Peace Prize, he gave the $54,000.00 award to the civil rights cause. Then he went on with his work, this time centering on the town of Selma, Alabama, where black persons were virtually denied the right to register and vote.

In the course of the Selma struggle, thousands were jailed, including Dr. King, himself, but still they continued to sing "We shall overcome." Two marches to Montgomery, the state capitol, met with impenetrable opposition; but the third, protected by Federal troups, made its way in triumph. After that, there were marches for free ballot boxes and desegregated schools and economic justice. But it was in a 1968 Memphis, Tennessee struggle for economic justice that Dr. King was felled by an assassin's bullet. Like the Lord whom he followed, he gave his life for his people.

Father Damien

Another person caught up in the compassionate spirit of Jesus was Joseph Damien de Veuster, born in Belgium in 1840. After he became a priest in the Congregation of the Sacred Heart of Jesus and Mary, he became known as Father Damien. His first field of service was on the Island of Hawaii. But in 1873, he felt urged to go and serve the colony of lepers on the nearby island of Molokai. At the time that he volunteered, there were 600 persons on that island suffering from leprosy, and until Father Damien went to them they had no one to help them.

For ten years, Father Damien worked untiringly for the residents of the leper colony. He ministered to their physical needs as well as to their spiritual needs. He helped the people build houses, churches, and roads. He organized two orphanages. He administered the sacraments of Baptism for the newborn, marriage for the adults, and extreme unction for the dying. Often, when a funeral occurred, it was Father Damien who not only officiated at the last rites but also dug the grave and interred the body. He counseled the troubled, heard confession from the penitent, celebrated Mass every Sunday and holyday, and even dressed the sores of the afflicted lepers.

Eventually Father Damien himself caught the dreaded disease of leprosy. Yet he wrote that he would not wish to be cured if the price of health meant leaving the work he was doing. Rather than desert the sick to whom he had ministered through the years, he chose to live out his life and die there in the colony he had learned to love and to serve. For the last six years of his life, he continued to serve the leper colony, though now aided by two other priests, two brothers, and several Franciscan sisters.

In all, Father Damien served the sick in the leper colony of Molokai for 16 years. He served those who needed him, the deprived and lowly people in sickness and isolation, following the spirit of the one he called Lord.

Parable of Parables

Who was this person whom Toyohiko Kagawa, Martin Luther King, Jr. and Father Damien followed in the patterning of their lives? What manner of man was he whose compassion has influenced men through 20 centuries and to the remotest parts of the world? The records tell of the way Jesus befriended such scorned and berated persons as Zacchaeus and Mary Magdalene. Records tell us, too, of his radical insistence on reconciliation and forgiveness. In his well-known Sermon on the Mount, Jesus said:

> "You have heard that it was said, 'An eye for an eye and a tooth for a tooth.' But I say to you, Do not resist one who is evil. But if anyone strikes you on the right cheek, turn to him the other also; and if anyone would sue you and take your coat, let him have your cloak as well . . . .
>
> You have heard it said, 'You shall love your neighbor and hate your enemy'. But I say to you, Love your enemies and pray for those who persecute you." (Matthew 5:38-40; 43-44)

Much that Jesus taught was expressed in the form of parables – stories of everyday life that epitomized larger and deeper meanings. An example of the parables of Jesus is the story of the Good Samaritan (Luke 10: 29-37), who tended to the wounds of a man beaten and lying by the roadside. A priest and a Levite had passed by the man, but the Samaritan, from a race that was frowned upon in Jesus' day, not only bound the man's wounds but also carried him to an inn where he could recover. The parable was Jesus' way of answering the question "Who is my neighbor?"

What, though, can men say to the ultimate question of the nature of Jesus. Was he fully human? Was he divine? Theologians in the Christian tradition have answered "yes" to both of the above questions. The mystery of the personhood of Jesus has been summed up in a parable of unknown origin:

> "Once upon a time, there was a marvelous inventor. He invented lights that go on and off automatically. He invented a substance out of which many things could be made. But he was lonely. So, in the course of time, he

invented a little creature, a manikin, capable of companionship with the inventor. The inventor made other such creatures.

But as long as the inventor controlled the manikins, the little creatures were nothing more than toys or playthings. The inventor realized that he must give his creatures free will, to choose their own course, whether wisely or foolishly. Only in freedom could the creatures become mature enough for real companionship with their inventor. So the inventor set his creatures free.

Tenderly the inventor watched the actions of the creatures. Sometimes he was very pleased with their choices. At other times he was severely grieved by the way they were hurting one another. From time to time the inventor would send spokesmen to live among the others, to proclaim a way of kindness, justice, and mercy. But the other creatures would seldom listen.

Finally, in the fullness of time, the inventor realized that messages and messengers were not enough. He realized that nothing would suffice except going, himself, to be one of his creatures. And so one day he 'emptied himself, taking the form of a servant, being born in the likeness of men.' (Philippians 2:7) He became one of his own creatures, living among them, to show the way."

The above parable is a way of explaining Christian theology in the simplest of terms. It is a way of explaining the Christian affirmation that Christ, though fully human, was also fully divine, in that the spirit of God dwelt fully in him.

The Trinity

Those who are not of the Christian faith are often bewildered by the Christian doctrine of the Trinity. This doctrine states that God is one but that there are three divine Persons in this one Godhead. These are the "Three Persons of the Trinity." Christians speak of God the Father, God the Son, and God the Holy Spirit, yet they mean one God. The three persons of the Trinity, for Christians, provide the way in which God reveals Himself to the world-namely, in His act of creating as Father, in His visit to earth as Jesus called Son, and in His abiding love called the Holy Spirit. The trinitarian view of theology is a way of explaining how God is known in His world; but never, in Christian theology, does this view imply more than one God.

The personal visit of God among men in Jesus is called the "Incarnation." It is affirmed in the name "Emmanuel," meaning "God with us" – a name which is conferred upon Jesus. Often, in Christian theology, there is reference to the "atonement" which is a word for bridging the gap between God and man. Atonement, when divided in syllables, can be read as "at-one-ment," meaning that in Jesus, God and man became one. Thereby all mankind was given the grace, or possibility, of living in harmony with God. The Incarnation, in Christian theology, is the antidote for sin, which has often been defined as man's separation from God. Man, alone, was not able to save himself from that sin, but God in Christ affected that reconciliation for him. As II Corinthians 5: 19 states: "God was in Christ reconciling the world to himself." In the eleventh century after Christ, a theologian by the name of Anselm of Canterbury explained the Incarnation in somewhat this way:

> "Only man needed the atonement.
> Only God could effect the atonement.
> Therefore God became man and thereby brought atonement."

Unity with Variety

Most Christians would agree with what we have said so far. But there is also a great deal of variety in the way Christianity is practiced, administered, and believed. The three historic traditions of Christendom are Roman Catholic, Eastern Orthodox, and Protestant. In Roman Catholicism, there are seven sacraments: Baptism, Confirmation, Penance, Eucharist, Anointing of the Sick, Holy Orders and Matrimony. These sacraments are administered by ordained priests, whose authority is part of a vested hierarchy of bishops, cardinals, and the Pope. The Pope, the titular head of the Roman Catholic Church, lives in the Vatican in Rome and when he speaks officially (*ex cathedra*) on matters of doctrine or morals his word is considered to be infallible. Eastern Orthodoxy also practices the seven sacraments, called mysteries, but finds its authority in the Bible and the Church Fathers, interpreted by the Church and guided by the Holy Spirit. Protestant Christianity basically practices only the two sacraments of Baptism and Eucharist, called Holy Communion. There are over 200 denominations within Protestant Christianity. Some of these denominations, such as the Methodists and Presbyterians, practice Baptism by the sprinkling of water on an infant's head as a symbol of his becoming a member of the church fellowship which is often called "The Body of Christ." Other denominations, such as Baptists and Disciples, practice Baptism by total immersion, and only for those old enough to understand the meaning of the event.

For all Christians, the Bible is the sacred literature, and it consists of both the Hebrew Bible (which Christians call the Old Testament) and 27 other books called the New Testament. These New Testament books consist of four Gospels or accounts of the life of Jesus, a history of the Early Church called "The Acts of the Apostles," a number of letters or epistles written mostly by St. Paul of Tarsus, and the Book of Revelation which is an apocalyptic interpretation of the ultimate reign of God.

The differences among the various traditions of Christianity have caused serious rifts, and even tragic wars at certain times and places. But the bright spot on the horizon is the new trend toward ecumenism – a mutual respect and recognition that is emerging today among the various churches throughout the world. Both the World Council of Churches and the Vatican Council Decree on Ecumenism have spoken decisively in the mid-twentieth century on behalf of inter-church dialogue. Many local churches and church organizations are now working together on projects that build healthy community relations. Among Protestant Christians there have been a number of denominational mergers, and many more are being explored. But perhaps more important than the ecumenical ventures of church organizations are the grass roots movements which are evidencing cooperation throughout the world. One writer said that the real beginning of the ecumenical movement was made when a Jewish rabbi, a Catholic priest, and a Protestant minister marched side by side on the road to Selma, Alabama in a concerted effort to win civil rights for the people of that area.

Holy days

The Sabbath for most Christians is on Sunday, the first day of the week. The change from the Jewish Sabbath on the seventh day of the week to the Christian Sabbath on the first day began with the event of the Resurrection, which was recorded as being on Sunday. The Resurrection is a Christian belief that Jesus could not be contained in the tomb, but arose to inspire and empower all his followers to newness of life. Therefore, in churches throughout the world, services of worship are held each Sunday. The worship procedure in each church ranges from the formal celebration of the Mass in Roman Catholic parishes to the more informal prayer, hymn-singing, and sermons of many Protestant churches. In some churches of more emotional expressiveness, there is spontaneous congregational participation along with much singing and rejoicing.

The Resurrection of Jesus is celebrated today also in an annual event called Easter, which for most churches is the first Sunday after the first full moon after the spring equinox. Often on Easter there are sunrise services in which the Resurrection is celebrated with singing, a message of hope, and decorations of spring flowers, especially lilies. In Roman Catholicism Easter is the culmination of the liturgical year and services at Eastertime sum up all of Christian theology. Children celebrate Easter with egg hunts in which they gather brightly colored eggs that have been hidden. The association of the egg and Easter stems from the coincidence of the Resurrection with ancient spring festivals. Yet the egg as a symbol for new life is not inappropriate for Easter.

Other events in the Church year include Pentecost, seven weeks after Easter, often considered the "birthday of the church." In the Book of Acts in the New Testament, the scene

Latin cross

Symbol for the Trinity

Toyohilko Kagawa, who patterned his life after Jesus of Nazareth, befriending the sick, the poor, the outcast, and working for social justice.

of the first Pentecost after the first Easter describes the followers of Jesus suddenly dramatically aware of the spirit of the risen Christ with them, and determined to go forth and spread the good news of all that had happened.

Christmas, the day on which the birthday of Jesus is celebrated, is also an annual event in Christendom. Christmas is the formal celebration of Jesus' Incarnation. Although the preoccupation with gifts and department store decorations often obscures the underlying meaning of this season, there is quietly underneath the exterior celebration an inner joy over the deep abiding love that came into the world on that first Christmas. Children who learn to re-enact the story of the birth of Jesus, in a humble stable with straw and animals, catch the feeling of warmth and wonder that is uniquely Christmas.

The fish is an ancient Christian symbol. The Greek letters IXTHUS stand for the first letters in the words: Jesus Christ, Son of God and Savior.

Discussion Questions on Christianity

1. In what way can Christianity be considered a revolutionary religion?
2. Imagine that you lived in the first century A.D. How would you describe the man Jesus?
3. If Jesus were alive in human form today, where do you think you would find him, and what do you think he would be doing?
4. Describe a modern Christian about whom you have read, or whom you know.
5. Describe the Christian belief in the Trinity.
6. What are the three main divisions within Christendom, and in what ways do they differ from one another?
7. What is the ecumenical movement? Do you know of any evidence of it in your neighborhood? Describe.
8. What are the main holy days in the Christian calendar, and how and why are they celebrated?
9. Does Christianity need more days of celebration? If you were to plan a new celebration, what would you plan? What kind of celebration? What mood and meaning would it express?
10. Pick one parable that Jesus told and re-tell it in your own words or re-tell it with a modern setting and a modern application of its meaning.

Bibliography on Christianity

A. **Books:**

Primary Source: *The Holy Bible*

Secondary Sources:

Cocagnac, A.M. *When I go to Mass.* New York: Macmillan, 1965.

Donovan, V. *Judaism and Christianity.* Glen Rock, N.J.: Paulist Press, 1963.

Fritz, Dorothy, *The Use of Symbolism in Christian Education.* Phila. Westminster Press, 1961.

Hunter, A.A., *Courage in Both Hands.* N.Y.: Fellowship of Reconciliation.

Johnson, J.W. *The Books of American Negro Spirituals.* New York: Viking Press, 1953.

Kagawa, Toyohiko. *Songs from the Slums.* New York: Abingdon Press, 1935.

Niebuhr, Hulda. *The One Story.* Philadelphia: Westminster Press, 1949.

Rest, Fredrick. *Our Christian Symbols.* Philadelphia: Christian Education Press, 1954.

Time-Life Editors. *I Have a Dream.* New York: Time-Life Books, 1968.

B. **Audio-visuals:**

Records:

Sister Germaine. "Songs of Salvation." F.E.L. Publications (22 E. Huron, Chicago, Ill. 60611

"Hymns for Now" Concordia Publishing House, 875 N. Dearborn St., Chicago, Ill. 60610

"Mahalia Jackson Sings the Best-Loved Hymns of Martin Luther King, Jr." Columbia Records

"Music for the Worship of God in the Twentieth Century." Scepter Records, 254 W. 54th St., N.Y., N.Y.

Ray Repp. "Mass for Young Americans." F.E.L. Publications, 22 E. Huron, Chicago, Ill. 60611

Paul Robeson. "Songs of my People." R.C.A. Victor Records, 1972.

Salli Terri and the Roger Wagner Chorale. "The Negro Spiritual." Promenade Series. Capitol Records, 1290 Avenue of the Americas, N.Y., N.Y. 10013

Filmstrips:

"Jesus and his Disciples." United Church Press, 1505 Race St., Philadelphia 19102

"Life of Christ" Part I and Part II. Ibid.

Film:

"Parable"–National Council of Churches of Christ in the U.S.A. (475 Riverside Drive, New York City.)

Islam

The youngest of the major living world religions is Islam. This religion is sometimes called "Mohammedanism" because its prophet and founder was named Mohammed (more accurately spelled Muhammad). But the prophet of the faith has made no claims to divinity, and the focus therefore in this religion is more accurately placed on The God, and man's surrender to him. The word "Islam" means "surrender," and followers of this faith are called "Muslims" because the word "Muslim" means "One who surrenders."

There is a sense in which Islam is not only the youngest but also the oldest of the world religions. It is youngest if you date it from its prophet's birth, or from the Hijrah, his migration from Mecca to Medina. But it is the oldest in the sense that the Muslims consider it to be of eternal origin. Also, the Arab people, among whom Muhammad was born, attribute their ancestry to the Patriarch Abraham, the same bold wanderer who is also considered the founding father of Judaism and Christianity. But Islam traces its ancestry in Abraham not through Isaac, as do Jews and Christians, but through Ishmael, who with his mother Hagar was sent away from Canaan after Isaac was born. The Book of Genesis, chapters 16 and 21 tells this story, and how Hagar found water for Ishmael even in the desert.

The Story of Muhammad

It was about 25 centuries after Ishmael, in the year 570 A.D., that the prophet Muhammad was born. The place of his birth was Mecca, in Arabia. Gambling, drinking, and a lucrative idol worship were the order of the day in Mecca at that time – to say nothing of a stratified economic society and a sort of "might makes right" law. Circumstances were crying for new leadership though the power structure was hardly ready to yield to a new voice. Yet the new voice came with the birth of Muhammad.

The Prophet Muhammad seemed destined to learn early of life's problems. His father died before he was born, and his mother died when the boy was only six years old. A grandfather cared for young Muhammad for two years but then also passed away. It remained for an uncle, Abu Talib, to take the boy into his care and to give him a place tending sheep. Thus from an early environment of personal loss and deprivation, this prophet-to-be developed a sensitivity to life and a searching quest for meaning out of seeming perplexity. His reputation as an honest man earned him the nick-name "Al Amin" which means "The Honest One."

Upon entering manhood, Muhammad went to work as a caravan leader. So able was he at his work that his reputation spread, and the owner of the caravans asked to meet him. The owner was the wealthy Khadijah, a woman 15 years older than Muhammad, but quite beautiful. The story goes that she fell in love with him, and sent notes suggesting that he marry her. Khadijah and Muhammad were married, and it turned out to be a lasting and happy match. Four daughters and three sons were born to them.

Whenever he had leisure time, Muhammad liked to wander in the cool caves of Mt. Hira and to meditate. One evening, during the month of Ramadan, while he was meditating in the cave, Muhammad felt a presence and believed that the Angel Gabriel was relating a message to him from the one God, whom he called "Allah," meaning "The God." Muhammad went back to his wife to relate the awe-inspiring event. Khadijah became convinced that indeed he had been chosen to relay a message to the people from the one God.

Muhammad continued to receive messages which he later dictated to his secretary, Zeid. These messages, written on stones, bones, leaves, or whatever material was handy, were later collected and arranged in the sacred literature of Islam called the Qur'an. That first message to Muhammad, now listed as Surah 96 of the Qur'an begins:

In the name of Allah, the Beneficent, the Merciful.

1. Read: In the name of thy Lord who createth,
2. Createth man from a clot.
3. Read: and thy Lord is the Most Bounteous,
4. Who teacheth by the pen,
5. Teacheth man that which he knew not.
6. Nay, but verily Man is rebellious
7. That he thinketh himself independent!
8. Lo! unto thy Lord is the return.

(Pickethall, 1953, pg. 445)

Meanwhile, in Mecca, Muhammad met with much opposition to his messages. In the first place, his message of uncompromising monotheism was a threat to those who made their living by managing some of the 360 shrines to polytheistic deities; in the second place, his moral regulations threatened the licentiousness of the day; and in the third place, the equality of all men which he proclaimed went against the grain of a rigid social and economic order. Thus Muhammad was not able at first to find many followers in Mecca.

But in the city of Yathrib (later called "al Medina," "the city"), some 200 miles away, there was a growing number of persons interested in Muhammad's message. Conflicting interests in that city seemed to call for a voice that could unify the people, and Muhammad was chosen as that voice. Actually, Muhammad's life was now in danger in Mecca, and utmost precaution had to be taken in order for the prophet to slip out of town and travel to al Medina. The flight to Medina, called the "Hijrah" or "Hegira," in the year 622, is considered the turning point in Muslim history, and it has become the year from which Muslims date their calendar.

At Medina, Muhammad became not only the spiritual but also the political leader of the people. His administration is noteworthy for its sense of justice. Even in his statesman's position Muhammad kept his humble touch. Tradition tells us that he continued to milk his own goat and to mend his own cloak! But there was a real financial problem now among Muhammad's forces. Some of the caravans of traders from Medina to Mecca had been plundered. It seemed only right to give equal treatment and therefore, Muhammad told some of his men the routes of caravans from Mecca, so that they, too, could be plundered and a balance achieved.

Soon the forces of Mecca recognized Muhammad as a threat and sent an army to attack Medina. In the first battle, the battle of Badr, Muhammad's forces won and the prophet proclaimed "Allah is with us." But in the second battle, the battle of Uhud, Muhammad's forces were conquered and the prophet was wounded. Now the followers asked him "Where is Allah now?"; Muhammad replied "Allah is testing us to see if we are as loyal in adversity as in victory." In the third battle a large ditch was formed and the forces of Medina won as the Meccans were bogged down. Over a period of several years, Muhammad gradually won over the city of Mecca. He returned for a pilgrimage and to set up a monotheistic worship, destroying the pagan shrines.

When Muhammad died in 632 A.D., at first the people refused to believe the news. But a staunch friend, Abu Bakr, stood up to say, "If you worship Muhammad, your god is dead. But if you worship Allah, whom Muhammad proclaimed, your God lives forever."

The Spread of Islam

From Mecca, Islam spread over Arabia and subsequently has spread so far and wide that today it commands 528,879,500 followers and is the second largest of the world religions. After Muhammad's death, the leaders of the religion were called Caliphs. Islam is gaining converts rapidly in many African countries today.

How does this religion, born of the desert caves and proclaimed by a prophet who could neither read nor write, affect the lives of so many millions? Undoubtedly its demand for an ordered prayer life, its proclamation of rewards and punishments in a life to come, and its sense of moral order is compelling to many persons.

The religious duties of a Muslim are summed up in the "Five Pillars" of Islam. These Pillars are:

1. **Recitation of the "Word of Witness"** "There is no god but Allah, and Muhammad is the messenger of Allah." This is the KALIMAH, the creed, and it must be pronounced *aloud*, it must be perfectly *understood*, believed in the *heart*, professed until *death*, recited *correctly*, and professed and declared *without hesitation.*

2. **Prayer five times a day**. Ritual prayer, called SALAT, is to take place at dawn, at midday, at mid-afternoon, at sundown, and at night. A specified order of position is called the *Rakah*, for which seven stages are ordered. The Friday noon *Salat* is the time for congregational worship at the mosque, and all able-bodied Muslim men are required to attend. In addition, there are free prayers called Du'a which Muslims utter as they feel the need. Leaders of prayer services are called Imams.

3. **Fasting from sun-up to sundown in the month of Ramadan**. During the daytime in this month, true Muslims neither eat, drink, nor engage in sexual intercourse. At the end of the month of Ramadan, there is a feast called the Id'l fitr at which presents are exchanged.

4. **The giving of alms**. In some Muslim countries there is a Zakat, or alms tax which is approximately 1/40th of a person's income. The money is used for many worthy causes including the alleviation of poverty. *Sadakat* is free giving of money to a charitable cause, often felt to bring merit to the giver in this life or the next.

5. **Pilgrimage to Mecca**. Once in a lifetime this is required of all who are physically and financially able. (Women can go but only if accompanied by a male relative.) The pilgrimage is to be made in the Hajj month, and consists of circumnambulation of the Kaaba (which houses the sacred stone) seven times, running between two hills to commemorate Hagar's search for water for Ishmael, and the hike to Mount Arafat, twelve miles

east of Mecca. On the return from the trip, pilgrims feast, and cast seven stones at each of three places to symbolize the stoning and rejection of Satan. Then they return to Mecca and make one final trip around the Kaaba. Some go on to Medina to visit Muhammad's tomb. A million pilgrims make this Hajj each year.

In addition to the Five Pillars of Islam, there are many commandments, including the "Ten Commandments" of the Hebrew Bible. There are also dietary commandments including the prohibition of alcohol, intoxicating drugs, and pork. Holy War in Islam is called *Jihad* and the theory behind it is that it is to be proclaimed only when the faith is attacked.

A good Muslim subscribes to five major theological tenets:

1. **Monotheism**. Muslims proclaim that there is only one God: Allah. Invisible, all-knowing, all-wise, all-powerful, beneficent, merciful – "Behold, Allah knoweth all and forgiveth whom he will!" According to an old legend, there are 99 names or attributes of God, and the hundredth only the camel knows! The story goes that Muhammad whispered the hundredth name to his camel, and to this day a camel holds his head high because of his secret information!

2. **Angels**. Muslims believe that unseen beings, of both good and bad influence, called angels and *jinn*, are assistants or hindrances to the will of Allah. Iblis (Satan), the fallen angel who refused to prostrate himself before Adam, is considered the cause of men's misdeeds. Every Muslim is thought to have two angels, one on the left and one on the right to record his bad and good deeds respectively. These recording angels will then present each man's record on the Day of Judgment.

3. **Prophets**. Muslims recognize many prophets, but believe that Muhammad is the "Seal" or last and final one who corrects the others and presents the message in its true form. Adam, Moses, Isaiah, Jesus . . . Muhammad are among the prophets who bring God's message, according to Muslim theology.

4. **Scriptures.** Muslims say *Qur'an* is the divinely inspired, divinely dictated word which corrects and supersedes all other scripture such as the Torah and the Gospel.

5. **Day of Judgment.** The Qur'an is very graphic in its description of the rewards and punishments meted out on the Day of Judgment. For the faithful, the Qur'an tells of paradise with underground streams of water and endless pleasures. But for the unfaithful it describes seven gates to hell where vast heat and a bottomless pit are among the tortures.

There is also a sixth tenet which pertains to predestination. According to Muslim theology, there is a tablet in heaven on which is written everything that is to come to pass, on the theory that God sees the future as well as the present. A number of passages in the Qur'an give the impression of a rigid predestination for man; yet other passages imply that God wills, but man is responsible if he departs from God's will. Theologians answer this seeming discrepancy by saying that Muhammad was a prophet, not a systematic theologian. Varying schools of thought have emerged, so that Jabrians hold to the absolute sovereignty of Allah while Quadrians say that it is wrong to attribute evil to Allah. To a Quadrian, God wills what is good, but man is free to follow or to reject God's will.

Sects in Islam

Islam is divided among a number of sects, though there is a concensus of agreement among orthodox muslims throughout Islam. The main sect of Islam is Sunni, encompassing 90 percent of the Muslims and proclaiming that Caliphs following Muhammad were chosen, not descended. Most other Muslims are of the Shi'a sect which maintains that the Caliph should be hereditarily descended from Muhammad and that leaders called "Imams" have special powers. Islam encompasses the whole of life, and does not generally promote asceticism. In fact a good Muslim can have four wives at the same time *if* he can maintain them and treat them equally. (Muhammad had ten wives at one time after Khadijah's death, but before the limitation of four wives.)

However, there grew up among the people of Islam a movement that is of a monastic type, with a mysticism that is not usual in the orthodox circles. Because these seekers usually wore white wool garments, they came to be known as Sufis (meaning white wool) and Sufism is the mystic movement in Islam. Literature of the Sufis is tender – it combines the strong relationship of man to one God that typifies all of Islam, with the deep feeling tone of one who merges his soul with the soul of the Infinite.

A mystic poem by Jalal al-Din Rumi of the thirteenth century gives us the flavor of mystic Islam with its burning passion of man for God:

The Shepherd's Prayer

Moses saw a shepherd on the way, crying, "O Lord Who choosest as Thou wilt,
Where art Thou, that I may serve Thee and sew Thy shoon and comb thy hair?
That I may wash Thy clothes and kill Thy lice and bring milk to Thee,
O worshipful One;
That I may kiss Thy little hand and rub Thy little feet and sweep Thy little room at bed-time."
On hearing these foolish words, Moses said, "Man, to whom are you speaking?
What babble! What blasphemy and raving! Stuff some cotton into your mouth!
Truly the friendship of a fool is enmity: the High God is not in want of suchlike service."
The shepherd rent his garment, heaved a sigh, and took his way to the wilderness.
Then came to Moses a Revelation: "Thou hast parted my servant from Me.
Wert thou sent as a prophet to unite or wert thou sent to sever?
I have bestowed on everyone a particular mode of worship,

I have given everyone a particular form of expression.
The idiom of Hindustan is excellent for Hindus; the idiom of Sind is excellent for the people of Sind;
I look not at tongue and speech, I look at the spirit and the inward feeling.
I look into the heart to see whether it be lowly, though the words uttered be not lowly.
Enough of phrases, conceits, and metaphors! I want burning, burning, burning; become familiar with that burning!
Light up a fire of love in thy soul, burn all thought and expression away!
O Moses, they that know the conventions are of one sort, they whose souls burn are another."
The religion of love is apart from all religions. The lovers of God have no religion but God alone.

(Stace, 1960, pg. 214-15)

Malcolm X

In recent years in the United States, a group of Muslims led by Elijah Muhammad developed a black separatist movement. Members, called "Black Muslims," have kept the rituals of orthodox Islam but have added their own emphasis of liberation for black people. To many oppressed persons, this new form of religion has come to be highly meaningful. One of its finest proponents was Malcolm Little, later known as Malcolm X because blacks in America cannot know their true ancestral names which were lost when slaves were brought to these shores from Africa.

In *The Autobiography of Malcolm X*, we read of the outrages this person suffered as a child and as a young man. Shortly before he was born his home was surrounded by the Ku Klux Klan. When he was only six, his father died a mysterious death that appeared to be murder but was attributed to suicide so that no insurance money could be collected. There followed poverty, the mental illness of Malcolm's mother, and the placing of the children in foster homes, so that family members were separated. In later years, in a desperate effort to make enough money for his family, Malcolm X became a "procurer," and when caught was imprisoned.

It was during his prison years that Malcolm X first became interested in the Black Muslim movement. His brothers and sisters in Detroit wrote him letters frequently, telling of their new interest in the movement led by "The Honorable Elijah Muhammad." The new religion had strong appeal because of the high standards of morality it commanded, including the abstinence from tobacco, alcohol, and drugs. Malcolm X wrote to Elijah Muhammad from prison, and received an answer from him, accompanied by a five-dollar bill. From then on, Malcolm X could not hear or read enough about the new religion which he now embraced wholeheartedly.

When finally out of prison, Malcolm X devoted his days to the spread of the Black Muslim religion. He visited his brother's home and was delighted by the orderliness of the ritual observances. He describes this Muslim home in this manner:

> "There was none of the morning confusion that exists in most homes. Wilfred, the father, the family protector and provider, was the first to rise. 'The father prepares the way for his family,' he said. He, then I, performed the morning ablutions. Next came Wilfred's wife, Ruth, and then their children, so that orderliness prevailed in the use of the bathroom.
>
> 'In the name of Allah, I perform the ablution,' the Muslim said aloud before washing first the right hand, then the left hand. The teeth were thoroughly brushed, followed by three rinsings of the mouth. The nostrils were rinsed out thrice. A shower then completed the whole body's purification in readiness for prayer.
>
> Each family member, even children upon meeting each other for that new day's first time, greeted softly and pleasantly 'As-Salaam-Alaikum' (the Arabic for 'Peace be

unto you'). 'Wa-Alaikum-Salaam' ('and unto you be peace') was the other's reply. Over and over again, the Muslim said in his own mind, 'Allahu-Akbar, Allahu-Akbar' ('Allah is the greatest').

The prayer rug is spread by Wilfred while the rest of the family purified themselves."

(Autobiography, 1964, pp. 193-4)

Malcolm X studied the rituals and scriptures of the Black Muslim movement and soon became an assistant minister in Detroit's Temple Number One. From there he moved on to minister to other temples, frequently visiting with Elijah Muhammad in Chicago. So great was the enthusiasm of Malcolm X for his newfound religion that he would recruit persons wherever he went. His bitterness for white oppressors found an expression in this separatist movement. But after some years, Malcolm X became disappointed in Elijah Muhammad, and decided to explore Islam from its original and orthodox sources.

It was on his pilgrimage to Mecca that Malcolm X came to see Islam in its wider context. Suddenly the religion which had meant so much to him as a separatist movement became even more meaningful as an expression of worldwide brotherhood. The complete equality of the pilgrims from all races on the "Hajj" was symbolic of the all-embracing view of true Islam.

Coming back to America, Malcolm X began proclaiming Islam in its global perspective. He still saw it as a way of life that had ultimate meaning for him, but he could no longer feel the need for complete black separatism. He advocated a strong black identity as a person of worth, and alertness to oppression wherever it abounded. But it was orthorox Islam that finally claimed the heart of Malcolm X. He spent the last of his days traveling over America, lecturing on college campuses, and spreading his message to other countries as well before a fanatic's bullet stilled his life.

Today small Muslim communities in America attract both black and white followers, while the Black Muslim group continues its separatist meetings. The ordered discipline of

The sacred ka'aba in the holy mosque in Mecca.

Malcolm X, famous American Muslim leader, during an address.

One ofthe minarets from which the call to prayer is given at the holy mosque in Mecca.

Muslim lives is appealing throughout the world. Perhaps it is best symbolized by the prayer rug that is the center of this whole way of life. As Malcolm X described it in his *Autobiography:*

> "I began to see what an important role the rug played in the overall cultural life of the Muslims. Each individual had a small prayer rug, and each man and wife, or each communal group, had a larger communal rug. These Muslims prayed on their rugs there in the compartment. Then they spread a tablecloth over the rug and ate, so the rug became the dining room. Removing the dishes and the cloth, they sat on the rug – a living room. Then they curl up and sleep on the rug – a bedroom . . . . Later, in Mecca, I would see yet another use of the rug. When any kind of dispute arose, someone who was respected highly and who was not involved would sit on the rug with the disputers around him, which made the rug a courtroom. In other instances it was a classroom." (Pg. 327)

Together with the five pillars of Islam and the five tenets of the faith, the prayer rug and the call to worship undergird the true Muslim's religious life. Five times a day in Muslim countries a Muezzin calls the faithful from the tall towers of the Mosque:

> "God is most Great!
> God is most great!
> I testify that there is no God but Allah.
> I testify that Muhammad is the prophet of Allah.
>
> Arise and pray; arise and pray.
> God is great.
> There is no God but Allah."

Discussion Questions on Islam

1. In what sense is Islam the youngest of the major world religions, and in what sense is it the oldest?
2. Why do Muslims date their calendar from the year 622 A.D.?
3. What obstacles did the Prophet Muhammad have to overcome in order to spread the religion of Islam in Mecca?
4. What are the Five Pillars of Islam?
5. Describe the Pilgrimage to Mecca.
6. What do Muslims believe about angels?
7. What is meant by the phrase "Muhammad is the Seal of the Prophets"?
8. What do Muslims believe about the Day of Judgment?
9. How are Sufis different from other Muslims?
10. What was the difference in the approach to Islam which Malcolm X took after his pilgrimage to Mecca?

Bibliography on Islam

A. **Books**

Primary Source:

The Meaning of the Glorious Koran. Translated by Mohammed Marmaduke Pickthall. New York: New American Library of World Literature, 1953.

Secondary sources:

Arberry, A.J. *Muslim Saints and Mystics.* New York: Mentor, 1960.

Cragg, Kenneth. *Alive to God: Muslim and Christian Prayer.* New York: Oxford University Press, 1970.

——— *The Call of the Minaret.* New York: Oxford University Press, 1964.

Gibb, H.A.R. *Mohammedanism.* New York: Oxford University Press, 1949.

Grube, Ernest J. *The World of Islam.* New York: McGraw Hill.

Padwick, Constance. *Muslim Devotions.* London: S.P.E.C., 1961.

Payne, R. The Holy Sword. *The Story of Islam from Muhammad to the Present.* New York: Collier, 1962.

Trimingham, T.S. *The Sufi Orders in Islam.* London: Oxford University Press, 1971.

Williams, John. *Islam.* New York: Simon and Schuster, 1961.

Wilson, J. Christy. *Introducing Islam.* New York: Friendship Press, 1959.

B. Audio-Visuals

Filmstrip:

"Islam" – Life Filmstrips, *The World's Great Religions* – series.

Tape Cassettes:

Islamic Productions International, Incorporated, P.O. Box 12202, St. Louis, Missouri 63157.

Principles of Muslim Prayer
adult version
children's version
Life History of the Prophet Muhammad
Sura Al-Satiha (Qur'an in arabic)

Films:

"The Moslem World: Beginnings and Growth" 11 minutes. Coronet Films, 65 E. South Water St., Chicago, Ill. 60601.

"Four Religions," New York: McGraw Hill.

Appendices

MSB

Flower

(A story which reflects the culture of three religions: Christianity, Zen Buddhism, and Shintoism.)

"Garden of Eden" was what the men from the nearby airbase called the Bonnells' backyard. The housing development, in which Lieutenant Irving Bonnell lived, was run-of-the-mill; the wonderland his wife had created, right outside their kitchen door, was close to paradise.

Irving had met and married Hanako during his service in Tokyo. Everyone who strolled through her garden agreed that the English translation of Hanako – Flower – suited the Japanese bride admirably. Flower accepted her new name happily – it sounded more American – and from the day of her marriage she had done all she could to adjust to the new ways of her husband and his countrymen. She had sacrificed religion, country, culture, and most difficult of all – family.

Fortunately Flower didn't have to give up her green thumb. Her magic touch gave the plants in her garden a certain character of their own. They didn't wait to be looked at. They peeked out and flirted with you; they wrapped their fragrance around you like a lasso and pulled you to them; their brilliant colors coaxed your eyes into dancing. Even the rocks, bushes and dwarf trees, without a single bloom, were artfully arranged. The breezes sighed gently through the leaves of the shrubbery and the beautiful shapes of the rocks soothed you. A tiny brook that wound through the development washed the feet of all the plants and sang them to sleep in the evening.

It was no coincidence that so many people happened to drop by at the Bonnells. At first they came out of curiosity– to see the Japanese bride – later they came to admire the artistry of her hands. A friend at the airbase once confided to Irving, "When I'm all wound up after a fight with my wife or a rough day at the base, a walk through your garden relaxes me better than a shot of whiskey."

The garden was Flower's own special refuge. She had been born with a love for flowers. Her Tokyo neighbors believed that the gods had endowed her with a special gift and claimed that the lilies in Japan never stopped crying from the day she left. Flower had a reason of her own for planting her American garden. This only reminder of the past strengthened her to bear a burden that was becoming intolerable. The time she spent in the garden helped her store up energy for her daily encounters with her husband's mother.

Flower might not have survived her lonely struggle had not the gods intervened and sent her help in the form of her sister, Miyuko. Was it the gods? Or should we call it "chance"? It doesn't matter. For Flower and Miyuko it was the gods who brought them together again – the gods and the death of their father.

"It was Father's last wish that I come to America and stay with you a short while," Miyuko said, as the sisters sat alone in the garden. "He asked that I carry his blessings to you."

"Would that he had come himself," Flower replied, "that I might sit by his side and place a flower in his hand and tell him of my sorrow." She looked at her sister, and tears welled in the eyes of both. "I cannot stay here any longer. I shall ask my husband for a divorce and return with you to Japan."

"Perhaps it is as well that Father is not here," her sister admonished. "He would grieve over your words."

"I cannot help it, Miyuko. Do you think I have not tried to carry this burden? Two years ago my husband asked me if his mother could live with us. I urged him to arrange this. Why shouldn't she live with us? Her husband was dead. She was alone. It was our duty to care for her. I wanted to have her as my own mother, to love her as my own blood; I am no longer Hanako, I am Flower Bonnell, and I belong to my husband and to his family."

"Then why do you talk of divorce?"

"Because if I stay I shall die . . . My husband's mother hates me, and I am slowly wilting in her shadow."

"And your husband?"

"Perhaps he does not know what is happening to me, for I have kept all this to myself. But he is aware that his mother does not like me. He thinks it will pass after we know each other better . . .

Miyuko rose from the bench and suggested that they walk a little. She chose the path along the brook, and as they proceeded she turned to her sister and said:

"When father warned you about hardships in America he also said, 'Everything can be overcome with love.'" . . .

Flower shrugged. "I am afraid my love is not as strong as Father's."

Miyuko's eye stopped at a small bed isolated by a circle of rocks. The flowers in it were stunted, the faded blossoms shriveled.

"What happened to this bed?" she asked.

"That belongs to my mother-in-law; she does not let me care for it. Some say she does this to spoil my garden, but that is not true. It is the hatred in her that causes everything she touches to wither and die. I *must* go away from her." . . .

After a moment Flower lifted her head, smiled at her sister, and said, "But enough of me. Tell me of Father's last days. I know only what you have written."

"Our father's face was peaceful as the sunbeams fell upon it for the last time. Our mountain lakes were never so calm. He spoke of you. I think he knew from your letters that you were suffering, though you never wrote directly about it. He made me promise to come to you to bring his final blessing and to encourage you to remain loyal to the gods.

"Yes, he knew you became a Christian after your marriage. He asked me to read to him from Christian books so he, too, could learn of your new religion. The more I read, the more he wanted to hear. I was rereading a story from the Christian Bible, when Father interrupted me, 'It is all true, my child. If I were young and did not know the gods as I know them now, I would give up the religion of my ancestors and become a Christian. But for me it is not necessary. The gods have revealed to me the mystery of love and given me the strength to forgive and to ask for forgiveness. When you see your sister, tell her that her father has walked the path that lies before her as a Christian and he will be waiting for her at the end.' "

Miyuko paused to take a flower out of her handbag. Though it was pressed and dried, the flower was not withered like the blossoms in Mrs. Bonnell's flower bed. Its colors, though faded, still showed sparks of life. The younger girl carefully handed the flower to her sister and continued:

"This was the last flower you put into Father's vase. He would not let it be taken to Shingawa. I did not know he had kept it until the night he died. 'Return this flower to your sister as a sign of my blessing,' he said. 'May she use it to bring happiness to her household and peace to my soul.' "

Irving Bonnell's mother was not a witch. Miyuko realized this when she met Mrs. Bonnell shortly before dinner. The darkness in the older woman's eyes reminded the young Japanese girl of her father. There was one difference – the muscles in Mrs. Bonnell's face were tense; deep lines were etched from the bridge of her nose upward; the darkness was imprisoned in her eyes. The unlined face of Miyuko's father showed that he had made peace with his darkness.

"She suffers very much," Miyuko told her sister.

Flower nodded. "It is true but I cannot find out why."

At the dinner table the lieutenant was in a light mood. "How do you like the American we've made of your sister? Sometimes I think I prefer her the way she was in Tokyo."

"How was that, Irving?" his mother asked.

"She used to hit me the way the sunrise hits Mount Fuji and makes everything happy. I never could wait to get off duty to visit her. If you think her garden here is something, you should have seen the one she had in Tokyo! I almost wanted to apologize to the flowers for taking her away from them."

"If you liked it so much, why didn't you stay?" Mrs. Bonnell's tone was barbed.

"Oh, come on, Mother, I'm only kidding."

"May we go into the living room for tea?" Flower suggested. "My sister has brought me a tea set you may like to see."

"Let Miyuko serve it the way she did in Tokyo," her husband added. "When you see this, Mother, you'll want her to give lessons to your woman's club."

Flower went into the kitchen and the others walked to the living room. Mrs. Bonnell took a place on the sofa next to Miyuko and made small talk.

"Weren't you afraid to travel such a distance alone?"

"The stewardess on the plane was very kind. I felt at ease."

"Do Japanese girls still marry Americans in Japan?"

The unexpected question puzzled Miyuko. Her "Yes" was guarded.

"I understand many Japanese brides have left their American husbands and returned to Japan."

"I know of only one or two," Miyuko answered.

"Why do you think they return?"

"I do not know. They must be unhappy here."

"But I thought Japanese wives were specialists in love – and loyalty."

"They must have been very unhappy here."

"Do you think your sister is unhappy in America?"

"Cut it out, Mother!" snapped Irving. "What kind of question is that?"

Flower entered the room, bearing a small brazier filled with burning charcoal. This she placed on a mat in the center of the floor. She bowed deeply to her sister, who stood up, returned the bow and walked directly to the kitchen. Flower took Miyuko's place on the sofa next to Mrs. Bonnell. "If you do not mind," she said, "my sister will perform the duties of hostess for the tea ceremony. In Japan this is a special art, and not everyone is skilled at it. Miyuko is one of the best."

Miyuko reentered the room carrying a pair of metal tongs. She walked gracefully, without haste, and placed the tongs beside the brazier. She returned to the kitchen twice more, and each time she placed the utensils carefully, exactly where each item belonged. After the third trip, she knelt on the floor before the brazier and sat back on her heels. Her body was erect yet relaxed.

Miyuko lifted the tongs and pecked at the charcoal. So carefully did she move the unburnt pieces from the edge to the center that she appeared to be creating an artistic design out of the smoldering lumps. Precisely she returned the tongs to their proper place.

Without a quiver her hands lifted the iron kettle slowly onto the grill. Flower and the lieutenant maintained the appropriate silence until the water bubbled into a boil. Mrs. Bonnell made no attempt to speak either. She appeared entranced by the graceful flowing movements of the Japanese girl—the way Miyuko dipped a bamboo spoon into the bowl of powdered green tea and transferred three spoonfuls (no one larger or smaller than the other) into the empty tea cup before her. Then she sank the long bamboo dipper deep into the kettle and drew it out overflowing with hot water. She held the dipper over the kettle for a moment, poured exactly one-third of the water over the tea powder in the cups and returned the rest to the kettle. She picked up the bamboo whisk that looked like a shaving brush, gripped it firmly yet without tension, and beat the mixture in the tea bowl as one would whip cream—until it was frothy. There was never the slightest haste. Miyuko's complete attention was focused on each movement. Her thoughts did not wander to the previous maneuver or to the one ahead. Mrs. Bonnell had the feeling that had she interrupted the girl at any point in the ceremony, she could have returned a week later and continued from the exact place she left off.

During the fifteen minutes of the tea ceremony the three watchers experienced a strange feeling. They were no longer aware of each other's presence. Tea was being prepared – they knew that; but Miyuko, the person preparing it, had disappeared. They heard only the "wind in the pines" – the bubbling water in the kettle – and they saw only the perfect harmony of movements leading to one goal – the preparation of a cup of green tea. All three awaited that tea with unrestrained anticipation.

Miyuko cupped the tea bowl in both hands, bowed and placed it before the lieutenant. He put the bowl on the palm of his left hand and, supporting the side of the bowl with his right hand, he sipped.

"Ah, Miyuko," Irving said with a smile, "not even in your beautiful Japan could the flavor of your tea excel this." She bowed, and he handed the bowl to his mother.

Mrs. Bonnell sipped from the bowl twice and complimented Miyuko: "I have never enjoyed waiting for my cup of tea as I have today." She continued to hold the bowl.

Her son whispered to her, "Mother, you're supposed to pass the bowl to Flower."

She turned and offered the bowl to her daughter-in-law. For a brief moment their eyes met. Flower was stunned. Is this the face of my husband's mother? The same darkness shadowed the older woman's eyes, but the tense lines in her face had disappeared. The turmoil had been replaced by tranquility. How like Father she looks, Flower thought.

Flower complimented her sister and drank the rest of the tea in the bowl. Then she helped her sister carry away the utensils. When they reached the kitchen, Flower asked, "Did you see her face? I have never seen such an expression before. It almost reminded me of Father."

"I noticed it when I first met her," Miyuko answered. "You have been away from Father too long – perhaps you do not remember."

"No, I could never have missed this before. Something happened to her during the tea ceremony – something that removed the hedge of thorns. Did you see? The tenseness in her face was gone! If only I could discover the hedge! I'd tear it up by its roots and burn it in the fire. If it were gone forever, Miyuko, I would have a mother again!"

"And your father," added her sister.

"But the hedge will grow back and the thorns will be sharper."

Flower was right. The hedge had grown back by the time the sisters returned to the living room; the lines furrowed more deeply than ever in Mrs. Bonnell's face. Her words pricked them sharply. "It's really not necessary to hide in the kitchen to talk behind our backs. You can speak in Japanese right before us, and we won't know what you really think of us."

The two sisters exchanged glances and did not speak. Flower took her place on the sofa, Miyuko on a stool.

"The tea was charming," Mrs. Bonnell said to Miyuko, but her insincerity made the girl understand her sister's comparison to a thorny hedge. She flinched as the older woman went on, "You must teach me the ceremony before you return to Japan. When do you expect to go back?"

"I have not thought about it," Miyuko replied. "Perhaps in a few weeks."

"You're welcome here as long as you wish to stay," her brother-in-law offered. "I won't be surprised if you never go back. When the bachelors at the base get a look at you, they'll fall like a ton of bricks."

"I do not understand what you mean," Miyuko said.

Flower tried to explain the expression to her in Japanese, but Mrs. Bonnell interrupted angrily, "Stop it! I don't want to hear that language in this house!"

"Mother, for God's sake, she's only trying to explain what I said!"

"I don't care. I don't want sneaky talk in my presence!"

There was a complete silence until Mrs. Bonnell, with an obvious effort, regained control of herself. This time she spoke slowly and distincly to Miyuko, "What my son means is that you have come here to get an American husband."

"I didn't say that!"

Mrs. Bonnell ignored her son's protest. "Isn't that the goal of every Japanese girl? They couldn't conquer us with their sneaky bombs but they're succeeding with their geisha girls!"

"It would be an honor to marry an American as kind as your son," Miyuko replied, "but that is not why I came to America. I wished only to visit my sister and . . . ."

"And take her back to Japan with you," Mrs. Bonnell finished the sentence for her.

"That isn't true," Flower protested.

"Don't lie to me! Go back, both of you! That's where you belong. That's where all Japanese belong. If only you had never left your country – none of you, ever. We would have been so happy . . . ." Mrs. Bonnell burst into tears and groped for a hankerchief.

Irving, by helpless grimaces and gestures, pleaded with the sisters to understand. No one knew what to say or do; they sat like puppets waiting for the master to pull the next string. In the background of the sobs that punctuated Mrs. Bonnell's tears could be heard the chirrup of crickets in the garden and from far off the drone of airplane engines in the night.

After what seemed an eternity, Mrs. Bonnell lowered her hands and stared toward the window. "What's that?" she asked.

All three strained to hear and see – there was nothing unusual.

"Do you hear them?" The woman's voice rose.

"Mother, it's only some planes from the base."

The planes were louder now. The wind was from the east and the planes had to fly over the Bonnell house for a proper landing.

"Yes, planes – planes . . ." his mother repeated. "Planes – Jap planes – coming in low. They're heading for the harbor – oh, Jim! Come home, Jim! Don't stay there; they'll get you – Jim!!"

Her misty eyes saw the sisters staring at her. But they were not gardener, not tea hostess, least of all daughter-in-law – they were two Japs!

The planes skimmed the rooftop of the house; the roar of the engines muffled the distraught woman's screams as a stormy sea drowns out the cry of a lone gull. The planes went on, taking their thunder with them, and Mrs. Bonnell buried her face in the cushion next to Flower's knee. "Jim, Jim – why did they come? Why did they come?" she sobbed.

Irving knelt beside his mother and stroked her hair. His wife sat unmoved, and the lieutenant knew he would have to tell her the story he had determined she should never hear.

"Jim was my father," he began. "Dad was on board a destroyer when the planes hit Pearl Harbor. He never knew what happened." Irving paused, but his hand never ceased the gentle caressing.

"I was only one at the time. Mother was very bitter." He shrugged, and for a moment his hand slowed.

"I guess I was wrong, but I made Mother promise never to tell you. I could understand how she felt, but I thought once she met you . . ." he shrugged helplessly. "Well, it didn't work."

Mrs. Bonnell straightened, gave a last sigh and wiped her eyes. "I'm glad it's out," she said. "You should never have asked me – it's been too much of a strain."

Wordlessly, Flower gazed at her. The girl rose, picked up the dried blossom her sister had given her and placed it gently in her mother-in-law's lap.

"Why?" Mrs. Bonnell asked, some of the old tension returning to her face. "Why have you always accepted my taunts in silence? It would have been so much easier to hate you, if you had only struck back. Even now you sit there calmly, as if nothing had happened; you give me a flower – why?"

Flower sighed, but her voice was filled with affection.

"In my heart I often wanted to retaliate – even to run away from you and my husband. I knew you disliked me, but try as I might I could not find out why. Now I understand and a cloud has lifted. Why should I wish to strike back at you or to leave you? It would give me no happiness, and it would dishonor the grave of my father."

"You never told me your father died," her husband said.

"I learned of his death only recently, and just this morning, Miyuko gave me the details. She came here because my dying father asked her to bring me his blessing."

For a woman who believed in observing the amenities Mrs. Bonnell proved sorely lacking in sympathy. She seemed almost to relish the news as she remarked: "At least your father lived long enough to enjoy his children. My son can't even remember what his father looked like!"

Miyuko could be still no longer. Calmly, but strongly, she spoke her feelings of love and pity.

"Ever since I met you this evening I have wondered about the expression in your eyes; it reminded me of my father. My sister mentioned this to me when we were alone in the kitchen, for she recognized it also. Now I know what this likeness is. You, like our father, suffered very much in life.

"Before my sister and I were old enough to talk, Father was severely burned. He was taken to a hospital in Tokyo, and there he remained until his death. You are right when you say that we were more fortunate than your son in having our father for many years. We were permitted to visit him, and we never missed a single day. Each moment at our father's bedside was precious to us. From his burned lips we learned about the gods and about life and death. He gave us courage to face life.

"Because of his love for us, we wished to bring happiness to his heart. Flower created this happiness through her garden, and every plant she grew was destined to take its place in the vase beside our father's bed. As for me, from the time I was able to hold a bowl in my hands, I performed the tea ceremony every day in my father's hospital room; I had no desire to prepare the green tea for anyone except our father.

"After our country's defeat in the war, we were able to find life worth living – thanks to him. When my sister asked him about marrying an American, he gave her his blessing and said, 'It is good that former enemies be united by love.'

"One month ago he died in that same hospital. The doctors said he lived all those years in great pain, but he never showed it to us. Perhaps this is why we were not frightened by the darkness in his eyes. When I performed the tea ceremony this evening, for some reason the darkness in your own eyes became as warm as our father's.

"At his funeral they held a special ceremony attended by many Japanese; your American ambassador to our country came. Father was the latest person to die as a result of the atomic bomb explosion on Hiroshima."

Miyuko became silent.

Mrs. Bonnell stared at the sisters. The lines around her eyes relaxed. She picked up the dry blossom lying in her lap and lifted it slowly until it touched her lips.

From *Deep Well* by Emil Paul John. Friendship Press.
Used by permission.

Gohei Saves His Village

(The following is a true story from Japan, reflecting Buddhist compassion.)

Kindly sixty-year-old Gohei, headman of his village, was alone in his house on the hilltop when it began to creak and shake. Feeling that this was something extraordinary, he stepped outside into the early evening twilight. The quake was not especially strong, but Gohei was filled with uneasiness. Never before had he experienced such a long earthquake nor heard such rumblings in the earth.

At first when he gazed from the village below to the beach and from the beach out to the distant horizon, the sea appeared as quiet as usual. Then the wind began to carry the waves away from the land. The water receded, leaving a wide sandy beach. Great rocks stood out black and bare as if the very depth of the earth were being uncovered. Gohei caught his breath in surprise. "That sea! That strange sea!" he exclaimed.

This was a tidal wave. The water flowing away from the land would pile up offshore until a mountain-like wave was formed and then come surging back again with scarcely a moment's warning.

The people in the village at the foot of the hill, quite unaware of what was happening, were absorbed in preparing for the next day's festival – a celebration of the abundant rice harvest. What could Gohei do to warn them? It was useless to call – they would not hear him – and there was no time to run down the hill.

His eyes rested on the golden shocks of grain, the rice harvest produced by blood and sweat and toilsome labor–a treasure almost as precious as life itself. "That's it," he thought. "With this I can save the people of my village."

Gohei ran into the house and immediately came back with a lighted torch. Panting, distraught, running about like a mad man, he set fire first to one and then another of the golden shocks. Then throwing away the torch, he stood, as in a trance, gazing out toward the sea.

"Go-n, Go-n!" The priests at the Buddhist temple on the mountain were swinging the suspended pole against the temple bell, giving the alarm of "Fire! Fire! Fire! *Go-n, Go-n, Go-n!"*

Hearing the alarm, the villagers paused in their preparations for the next day's festival and looked up the hill slope. "There's a fire," they cried out. "It's at our good Gohei's place. What's happened, I wonder? We must put it out! Come, bring buckets and poles!"

Men, women, children, old people, ran up the hill crying out, "Come now. Hurry! Hurry!"

Gohei stood motionless watching the file of people stretched out like a rope along the narrow path. The four hundred people of his village were hurrying up the hill, but to Gohei it seemed as if they were creeping along like ants. In suspense his heart cried out to them, "Make haste!"

At last twenty of the vigorous men reached the top and ran to put out the blazing fires that would soon consume that year's harvest. Calling loudly, Gohei stopped them, "Don't put out the fire," he said, "until all the people of the village are here. A terrible thing has happened!"

"Wha–wha–what has happened, Gohei?" they questioned.

"Soon, very soon, you'll understand," he said. "Are all the people of the village here? 256, 258, 300, 400." Bending down his fingers to keep track, he counted the people as assembled. "All are here, aren't they? There is no one missing?" he questioned insistently.

"Well, there's the reason for the fire! Look! Look!" Gohei pointed toward the sea. In spite of the dusky twilight, far off on the sea a thin dark line could be seen. As they watched, the line thickened and advanced with an amazing speed.

"A tidal wave!" the people gasped.

The points of the waves, like the tips of thousands of arrows in the hands of a charging army, swept toward the shore with a roar like that of a hundred claps of thunder. The mountain-like wall advanced before their very eyes.

"Go-o-o———Go-o-o———Go-o-o———Ba-n!" and the great wave broke. Houses, bridges, everything disappeared as if suddenly immersed in a huge caldron. The people watched the terrible boiling white sea storm wildly over the village.

No one could utter a word. While the wind fanned the burning rice to a blaze that lightened up the deepening dusk, the people stood transfixed, looking down at the sea that had swept away their houses.

Not until a cold wind blowing in from the ocean aroused them from their stupor did they realize what Gohei had done for them. Then without a word they knelt before him. Tears of thankfulness ran down his cheeks. He had accomplished the thing he had set out to do.

Friendship Press. Used by permission.

General Bibliography

(Books pertaining to one religion only are listed in the bibliographies at the end of the pertinent chapters, and are not repeated here.)

A. Books on World Religions

The Bible Reader, An Interfaith Interpretation. Walter M. Abbot, S.J.; Rabbi Arthur Gilbert; Rolfe Lanier Hunt; J. Carter Swaim. New York: Bruce Books, 1969.

Anti-Defamation League of B'nai Brith. *A Bibliography on Judaism and Jewish–Christian Relations.* 315 Lexington Avenue, New York, New York, 1966.

Bach, Marcus. *Major Religions of the World.* New York: Abingdon Press, 1959.

Bouguet, A.C. *Comparative Religions.* Baltimore: Penguin Books, 1961.

Bradley, David. *Circles of Faith.* New York: Abingdon Press, 1966.

Fitch, Florence. *One God, the Ways We Worship Him.* New York: Lothrop, Lee, and Shepard, 1944.

———. *Their Search for God: Ways of Worship in the Orient.* New York: Lothrop, Lee, and Shepard, 1947.

Gaer, Joseph. *How the Great Religions Began.* New York: Signet Books, 1956.

John, Emil Paul. *Deep Well.* New York: Friendship Press, 1967.

Mbitl, John. *African Religions and Philosophy.* Garden City, New York: Doubleday and Company, 1969.

McWhirter and Hawkinson. *Games Enjoyed By Children Around the World.* Philadelphia: A.M. Friends Service Commission, 1970.

Millen, Nina. *Children's Games from Many Lands.* New York: Friendship Press, 1943.

O'Dea, Thomas. *The Sociology of Religion.* Englewood Cliffs, N.J.: Prentice-Hall, Inc., 1966.

Ross, Floyd, and Hills, T. *The Great Religion by Which Men Live.* New York: Fawcett, 1963.

Ross, Nancy W. *Three Ways of Islam Wisdom.* New York: Simon and Schuster, 1966.

Satprakashananda. *The Use of Symbols in Religion.* 205 S. Skinker Boulevard, St. Louis: Vedanta Society, 1970.

Schoeps, Hans-Joachim. *The Religions of Mankind.* Garden City, New York: Anchor Books, 1961.

Scoville, Myra. *The World's Children in Pictures: Ways they Worship.* New York: Friendship Press.

Santayana, George. *The Life of Reason: Reason in Religion.* Vol. 3. New York: Charles Scribner's Sons, 1905.

Smith, Huston. *The Religions of Man.* New York: Harper and Brothers, 1958.

Smith, Wilfred Cantwell. *The Faiths of Other Men.* New York: Harper Torchbooks, 1963.

Stace, Walter. *The Teaching of the Mystics.* New York: New American Library, Mentor Books, 1960.

Stowe, David M. *When Faith Meets Faith.* New York: Friendship Press, 1963.

Terrien, Samuel, *The Golden Bible Atlas.* New York: Golden Press, 1964.

The Whole World Singing. New York: Friendship Press, 1950.

The World's Great Religions. New York: Time Incorporated, 1957.

The World's Great Religions. Special Edition for Young Readers. New York: Golden Press, 1958.

Wach, Joachim, *Types of Religious Experience, Christian and Non-Christian.* Chicago: University of Chicago Press, 1951.

Wolcott, Leonard and Carolyn. *Religions Around the World.* New York: Abingdon Press, 1967.

B. Books on Religion and Public Education

American Association of School Administrators. *Religion in the Public Schools.* Washington, D.C.: AASA, 1964.

Boles, Donald. *The Bible, Religion, and the Public Schools.* New York: Collier Books, 1963.

Duker, Sam. *The Public Schools and Religion; The Legal Context.* New York: Harper and Row, 1966.

Frommer, Arthur. *The Bible and the Public Schools.* New York: Liberal Press Books, 1963.

Little, Lawrence. *Religion and Public Education: A Bibliography.* Pittsburgh, Pennsylvania: University of Pittsburgh, 1966.

Little, Lawrence. *Religion in The Social Studies.* New York: National Conference of Christians and Jews, 43 W. 57th Street, New York, New York, 1966.

McCluskey, Neil, S.J. *Catholic Viewpoint on Education.* Garden City, New York: Doubleday and Company, 1962.

Michaelsen, Robert. *Piety in the Public School.* New York: MacMillan, 1970.

Panoch, T. and Barr, D. *Religion Goes to School.* New York: Harper and Row, 1968.

Pfeiffer, Leo. *Church, State and Freedom.* Boston: The Beacon Press, 1953.

Phenix, Philip. *Education and the Worship of God.* Philadelphia: Westminister Press, 1966.

Religious Education Association. *Religion and Public School Curriculum.* 545 West 111th Street, New York, 1973.

C. Audio Visuals

Color Slides:

"Man and His Gods: An Inquiry into the Nature of Religion." White Plains, New York: The Center for Humanities, Inc.

Eleven slide lectures "The Religions of Eastern Peoples" Sheikh Publications, 5 Beekman St., New York City.

Filmstrips:

African Religions. Bailey Films, Inc. 6509 DeLongpre Ave., Hollywood, Calif. 90028.

From Out of the Desert. Sound filmstrips on Judaism, Christianity, Islam. St. Louis, Missouri, Concordia, 1973.

Religions Around the World. Society for Visual Education. 1345 Diversey Parkway, Chicago, Ill. 60614.

Religions of Black Africans. Society for Visual Education, 1345 Diversey Parkway, Chicago, Illinois 60614.

Religions of Our World Neighbors. Family Filmstrips.

The World's Great Religions.–Filmstrip series. New York: Time-Life, Incorporated. Rockefeller Center, New York, New York, 10020.

Films:

Four Religions.–(B&W) 60 Min. Hinduism, Buddhism, Islam, Christianity. McGraw Hill, 330 W. 42nd Street, New York, New York, 1961.

Major Religions of the World.–(B&W) 20 Min. Encyclopedia Britannica, 425 N. Michigan Ave., Chicago, Ill. 60611.

North American Indians. B.F.A. Educational Media, Santa Monica, Calif. (2211 Michigan Ave.)

World Religions.–6 half hour films or video tapes. 20 Min. tapes for teachers. Ontario Educational Communications Authority, 2180 Yonge Street, Toronto, Ontario, Canada, M 4S 2 C1.

Cassette Tapes:

The Living Religions of the World. 10 tapes on world religions by Dr. Marcus Bach. $4.00 apiece. Unity Book Store, Unity Village, Missouri.

D. **Curricula on World Religions for Public Schools**

Asia: Asian Studies Curriculum Project. Berkeley, Calif. Palo Alto, Calif: Field Education Publication.

A Sequential Curriculum on Anthropology. Athens, Georgia: University of Georgia.

Communities Around the World. Minnesota Social Studies Curriculum Project. Minneapolis: University of Minnesota (350a Piek Hall).

God and Government. (Amherst Project) Menlo Park, Calif.: Addison-Wesley Publishing Co.

God and Man Narratives. Lincoln, Nebraska: University of Nebraska Press.

On Teaching the Bible as Literature. Ackerman, J.S. Bloomington, Indiana: University Press, 1970.

Religion in Elementary Social Studies,. Florida State University at Tallahassee.

Religious Freedom: Minority Faiths and Majority Rule. Social Studies Project of Harvard Universtiy. Columbus, Ohio: American Education Publication, 1967.

Religious Issues in American Culture, Religious Issues in Western Civilization, and Religious Issues in World Cultures. Spivey, R.A.; Gustad, E.S.; Allen, R.F., Menlo Park, Calif.: Addison-Wesley Publishing Co., 1972.

Religious Literature of the West. Whitney, J.R. And Howe, Susan. Minneapolis, Minnesota: Augsburg Publishing House, 1972.

Religious-Philosophical Systems. Chicago: Rand–McNally and Co.

Social Science Program. Educational Research Council of America. Boston: Allyn and Bacon (K-12, religion is one of six themes).

The Garden and the Wilderness, and *The Temple and the Ruin*. Lee, A.A. and Lee, Hope, A. New York: Harcourt Brace Jovanovich, 1973.

The Image of the Jew in Literature and Jews and their Religion. New York: Anti-Defamation League (315 Lexington Ave.).

The Sociology of Religion. Yinger, M.S. American Sociological Association.

Trailmarks of Liberty. Law in American Society Foundation. Boston: Houghton-Mifflin. (Elementary & Secondary).

World Religions. Ontario Department of Education, Senior Division, Montreal, Canada, 1971.

Films:

"Learning About Religion in American History Courses"

"Learning About Religion in Social Issues Courses"

"Learning About Religion in World Cultures Courses"

"The Supreme Court Speaks: Learning About Religion in the Public Schools." (Four films for teachers and parents, with accompanying booklets for each film) (Spivey and Allen, Florida State University, Tallahassee.)

Key to Glossary Pronunciation

Ā as in *fate, acorn*
Ä as in *father*
A as in *at*
Ç as in *chord*
C̈ as in *can*
Ē as in *equal, be*
Ë as in *her*
E as in *met*
Ġ as in *gem*
G as in *go*
Ī as in *ice, pine*
Ï as in *clique, marine*
I as in *it, pin*
Ō as in *note, so*
Ö as in *move, prove*
O as in *not, hot*
Ū as in *use, music*
Ü as in *rule*
U as in *up*

The accent mark (′) is on the accented syllable. If there is a secondary accent, it is marked with (″).

Glossary

Ā′bräham: Ancient sojourner from Haran to Canaan, described in Genesis; father of Isaac and Ishmael and hence progenitor of Judaism, Christianity, and Islam.

Äbü′ Bakr″: Staunch supporter of Muhammad and first Caliph of Islam.

Äbü′ Tälib″: Uncle of Muhammad, with whom the boy lived until manhood.

Ägäm′äs: Sacred scriptures to the Jains; term refers to sermons of Mahavira.

Ämäteräsü-ōmi-kämi: Sun goddess in Shintoism, formerly considered progenitress of Japanese imperial family and central figure of Shinto worship.

Ämidä: Japanese name for the spirit of the Eternal Buddha who is believed to save those of faith and lead them to the "pure land" that leads to Nirvana.

Ánalects: Writings of Confucius.

Ānättä: Doctrine in Buddhism that the soul cannot be said to exist.

Änicçä: Buddhist term for the impermanence of life.

Är'hät: A monk in Theraveda Buddhism who is seeking to earn salvation.

Ätmän: A word for the human soul in Hinduism; inseparable from Brahman.

Ävätärä: An incarnation or human manifestation of God or a god in Hinduism.

Bādŕ: First battle in war between Mecca and Medina in which Muslims were triumphant.

Bhägäväd Gitä: "The Song of God"—a sacred scripture in Hinduism, part of a longer epic.

Bhäkti: A yogi who realizes God through love.

Bible: Sacred scripture for Jews, Christians, and Muslims.

Bōdhidhärmä: The master who brought the strand of Buddhism from India which became Chan in China and Zen in Japan.

Bōdhisattvä: A Japanese Buddhist who has earned Nirvana but does not accept it; rather this person keeps working toward the goal that all persons eventually be prepared for Nirvana.

Brähmä: The creator form or manifestation of Brahman in Hinduism; in a trinity with Vishnu and Shiva.

Brähmän: The name for God or the Ultimate Reality in Hinduism.

Brähmin: A person of the highest caste in Hinduism; seer or priest.

Bübër, Martin: A modern Jewish theologian (1878-1967); author of *I and Thou*.

Caste: Order of society to which one is born in India. There are four main castes (Brahmin, Kshatrya, Vaisya, and Shudra) but many sub-castes.

Chän: Form of Buddhism in China which became Zen in Japan.

Chrīst: Title applied to Jesus of Nazareth, meaning "The Anointed One," "The Chosen One."

Christmas: The celebration of the birthday of Jesus.

Chōmetz: Leavened bread, hunted and destroyed in households preparing for the Jewish Passover celebration.

Chuang Tzü (Jwang Dz): A great Chinese Taoist following Lao Tzu (369-286 B.C.).

Confūcius: Latinized name for K'ung-Fu-Tzu (551-479 B.C.); founder of Confucianism.

Dāmien, Rev. Joseph Damien DeVeuster: Roman Catholic priest who gave his life serving lepers on the island of Molokai (1840-1888).

Ditch: Battle of Ditch—final battle between Mecca and Medina in which Muslim forces triumphed.

Dreydel: A small top with Hebrew letters on its four sides; used in a Hanukkah game.

Dü'a: Spontaneous prayers of Islam.

Durga Pügä: A worship and celebration in India in the fall of the year when clay statues are made, honored, and then thrown into the river.

Ēaster: Christian celebration of the Resurrection of Jesus from the dead.

Ēastern Ōrthōdox: Branch of Christendom separated from the Roman Catholic Church in 1054.

Esthër: Heroine of the biblical Book of Esther; celebrated during the Jewish festival of Purim.

Exōdus: Event in Jewish history whereby Hebrew slaves were led from Egypt into freedom; viewed by Jews as a saving act of God for His people.

Gäshō: The act of bowing before the altar in a Japanese Buddhist temple.

Gäthäs: Buddhist scriptures (sutras) in hymn or verse form.

Gaútämä, Siddhärthä: (560-480 B.C.) Founding figure of Buddhism; believed to have become the Buddha, the Enlightened One.

Gnana (Gyänä́): Form of Yoga in which the yogi realizes God through wisdom.

Hāgä́r: Abraham's servant and mother of Ishmael; considered ancestor to Arabian inhabitants of Mecca among whom Muhammad was born.

Häggä́däh: A recounting of a story in Judaism, specifically the Passover at the Seder meal.

Haíkū: Form of Japanese poetry consisting of three lines, with five syllables in the first line, seven in the second, and five in the third.

Ḥä́nükkäh (Chanuka): Jewish eight-day celebration of the oil that burned for eight days in the Temple following the victory of the Maccabees over the Syrians.

Hā́man: Villain in the story of Esther; hissed and booed at Jewish Purim observance.

Härō̆seth: Mixture of wine, apples, and nuts to represent the mortar handled during Jewish slavery in Egypt.

Hä́sidism: Jewish school of thought stressing love, joy, and humility.

Hävdä́läh: Special prayer at closing of the Jewish Sabbath; a candle used on the occasion.

Heschel, Abraham: Modern Jewish theologian (1908-1973).

Hī́jrä (Hegira): Muhammad's flight from Mecca to Medina in 622 A.D.

Hinäyä́nä (Theravada): Form of Buddhism prevalent in southeast Asia (Burma, Sri Lanka, Thailand).

Hōndō: A temple hall in Japanese Buddhism.

I Ching (pronounced E Jing): The Book of Changes–**systems of broken** (*yin*) and unbroken (*yang*) lines in trigrams and hexagrams–often used as guides in Chinese decision making.

Ïkebä́nä (Ē-kay-bah-nah): The Japanese art of flower arranging.

Ïmäm: A Muslim spiritual leader.

Índüs: River in India along which bards first sung chants (Vedas) of Hinduism.

Īsaac: Son of Abraham and Sarah; ancestor of Jews and Christians.

Ishmäel: Son of Abraham and Hagar; ancestor of Muslims.

Jain (Jan): A sect which emerged from Hinduism; stresses complete nonviolence and absolute protection of animals.

Jēsus: Revered by Christians as the divine, only begotten Son of God the Father; proclaimed "the Christ."

Jïhad: Holy war in Islam; proclaimed when the faith is attacked.

Jūjitsü: Art of self-defense related to Japanese Buddhism.

Kääbä: Sacred square edifice which Muslim pilgrims circumnambulate in Mecca, and toward which all Muslims face in prayer.

Kägäwä, Tōyōhïkō: Japanese Christian who lived among and served the poor.

Kärmä: Law of just retribution; type of yogi who seeks to realize God through good deeds.

Khädījäh: Wife of the Prophet Muhammad.

Kshätrïyä: Cast of social order in India pertaining to warriors, nobles, and rulers.

King, Martin Lüther, Jr.: Baptist minister who gave his life to further cause of civil rights for blacks (1929-1968).

Köän: Question used in Zen Buddhism to goad devotees to enlightenment.

Köran (Qur'an): Sacred scripture of the Muslims.

Lāō Tzu (Laō-Dz): "Grand Old Master", born around 630 B.C.; considered to be the founder of Taoism.

Latkēs: Potato pancakes often served during the Jewish season of Hanukkah.

Lōtus: Sacred symbol of Hinduism; also name of a special meditation position.

Lēvīte: Member of an ancient Jewish holy order who officiated as a priest; descendants of Levi.

Mähävírä: (Vardhamana) A founder of Jainism in India (596-427 B.C.).

Mähäyáñä: Form of Buddhism prevalent in China, Japan, Korea, and Viet Nam.

Malćolm X: (Malcolm Little) Ardent proponent of Black Muslims, later orthodox Muslim (1925-1965).

Mätźō: Unleavened bread served during Jewish Passover.

Mäýä: Hindu term for the illusory appearances of life which cover the realities.

Mećca: Sacred city of Islam; birthplace of Muhammad.

Meńcius: Follower of Confucius who expounded upon his ideas (370-290 B.C.).

Menṓräh: Candle holder used in Jewish worship; seven candles usually; Hanukkah menorah has eight plus a lighter.

Menúhäh: Tranquility, serenity, peace and repose of the Jewish Sabbath.

Mezǘzäh: Small box containing fifteen verses of the Torah affixed to Jewish doorposts.

Mill: Buddhist prayer wheel used in Tibet.

Mṓkshä: (Mukti) Hindu term for arriving at the summit of life where the sould does not need to be born into another body but merges with the soul of God.

Mṓrdecai: Hero of the story of Esther; celebrated at Jewish Purim.

Mosque: Place of worship in Islam.

Müeźzin: Person who gives the call to prayer in Islam.

Mühámmäd: Prophet of Islam considered to be the final prophet, the "Seal of the Prophets," (570-632 A.D.).

Ńanak: Founder of Sikhism in the 15th century A.D. (1469-1504).

N̈ichïren Shōshū: Sect of Japanese Mahayana Buddhism.

Nirväńä: The goal of life in Buddhism; eternal absence of desire; extinguishment of the flame of personal aspiration, and the end of all pain.

Ō-Bōn Ōdṓr̈i: Dance festival held in Japanese Buddhist temples in July and August to honor the recently dead.

Ōjüźü: Prayer beads that encircle wrists in some forms of Japanese Buddhist worship.

ŌM: Symbol of Hinduism.

Ōrïgäḿï: Japanese art of paper folding.

Parïnirväńä: The Nirvana of eternity achieved after death.

Passṓvër: Jewish eight-day celebration in memory of the ancient event when the Hebrews were spared the plagues before departing from slavery in Egypt (Celebrated for 7 days in Reform Judaism).

Peńtecost: Christian celebration of the indwelling of the Holy Spirit and the "birthday of the Church"; fifty days after Easter.

Prótestant: Christians of various denominations whose origins first involved some form of "protest" against Roman Catholicism (1517 A.D.) and other denominations begun at later times because of various interpretations of Christianity.

Pügȧ: A worship experience of festivities in Hinduism.

Pūŕim: Jewish celebration of the story of Esther.

Qur'äń (Koran): Sacred scripture of the Muslims.

Rä́hülä: Son of Siddhartha Gautama.

Rä́jä: A Yoga discipline centering around spiritual exercises and physical positions.

Räḱäh: Seven-step prayer position order for formal prayers in Islam.

Rä́mädan: Month on the Islamic calendar set aside for daytime fasting.

Rämä́yänä: Epic in Hindu literature telling of Rama, avatar of Vishnu.

Rēincarnā́tion: Belief that the human sould is reborn into a new body after death.

Resurrećtion: Christian doctrine that Jesus was raised from the dead and will draw men to himself; Christian belief in personal resurrection after death.

Roman Catholic Church: Chronologically, the first Church to organize Christian belief and liturgy; the body of Christians recognizing the Pope as Vicar of Christ on earth.

Rōsh Hōshä́nä: Jewish observance of the beginning of a new year.

Sab́bath: A weekly day of rest in Judaism and Christianity; a holy day; seventh day of week for Jews and first day for Christians.

Sädäkō Säsäkï: Young Japanese girl, victim of the bombing of Hiroshima who set about to fold a thousand paper cranes to wish peace to the world.

Sälät́: Formal prayer time in Islam; Friday noon service of worship.

Sämädhḯ: Complete absorption in Hindu meditation; worshipper realizes one-ness with God.

Sämsárä: The round of birth, life, death, and rebirth in Hindu theology.

Sänyä́sï (Sun-yä́-sē): A person in the fourth stage of life in Hinduism, a wanderer, liberated from all worldly cares.

Sätōrï: The flash of inspiration in Zen Buddhism.

Sedér: Special order of Passover services in Judaism.

Shäb́bät: Jewish name for Sabbath.

Shäḿos: Lighter candle in Jewish Menorah.

Shävǘos: Jewish holy day celebrating Pentecost, seven weeks after Passover; the honoring of the giving of the Ten Commandments and also the first fruits of the harvest.

Shïä́: Sect of Islam proclaiming Ali as first Caliph and seeing special divine powers in the imams (leaders).

Shin Bý̈u: Ceremony celebrating the "going forth" of Gautama from luxury to a life of detachment.

Shḯvä: The destroyer form of god in Hinduism, part of the Hindu trinity.

Shṓfär: Ram's horn blown to signal the beginning of a new year in Judaism.

Simkhäs Tōräh: Jewish celebration marking the end of one year's study of Torah and the beginning again for another year.

Süccoth (Sükkot): Festival of Booths or Tabernacles; thanksgiving feast for harvest and for provision of food to the Hebrews in the wilderness.

Sūdra (Shūdra): Lowest caste in Hindu social order.

Süfï: A monastic in Islam, usually with mystic theology.

Sümï-e (Sümï-ā): Japanese art of ink brush painting.

Sünnï: Sect in Islam stressing Abu Bakr as first Caliph.

Süträs: Buddhist scriptures; sermons or discourses of the Buddha.

Swämi: A Hindu holy man, teacher, or priest.

Tagōre, Rabindränath: Indian writer (1861-1941); winner of the Nobel Prize.

Taichï (Tai-gee): Symbol of Taoism; circle divided into light and dark halves.

Tai Chi Ch'uan (Tai-gee-jwan): Movement exercises that express the philosophy of Taoism with the whole body.

Tao Te Ching (Dow de Jing): Scripture of Taoism.

Therävādä: Cf. Hinayana Buddhism.

Tōräh: First five books of the Bible—written on scrolls for Jewish worship.

Tōrïï: Special gateway arches to Shinto shrines.

Transmigration: Doctrine that a soul passes from life in one body into life in a new body, either of another person or an animal or plant.

Trinity: Christian doctrine of One God manifest in Father, Son, and Holy Spirit.

Tripitäkä: Three Baskets of Wisdom—scriptures of Buddhism.

Ühüd: Second battle between Mecca and Medina.

Üpänishäds: Sacred scriptures of Hinduism, growing from commentaries on the Vedas.

Vaisyä: One of the castes in the Hindu social structure; above shudras, below kshatriyas.

Vedäntä: "End of the Vedas"–organizations stressing the philosophical side of Hinduism.

Védäs: Sacred scriptures of Hinduism.

Wäbï: Japanese flower arranging in "quiet taste" for tea ceremony.

Wü Wēi: Doctrine of "creative quietude" in Taoism.

Yang: Light side of *Tai Chi*

Yäsōdhärä: Wife of Siddhartha Gautama.

Yätrïb: City where Muhammad went f;om Mecca to proclaim his message; later called Al Medina meaning "The City".

Yin: Dark side of the *Tai Chi.*

Yōga: A Hindu spiritual discipline designed to help man realize God–to bring himself into unity with the Ultimate Reality.

Yōgï: A person who practices yoga.

Yom Kippür: Jewish holyday of repentance.

Zäzen: Special form of Zen Buddhist meditation.

Zen: Form of Buddhism relying not on intellect but on a flash of intuition which leads to *satori* (enlightenment).

Credits

Quotations to be credited are listed in the order of appearance in the text.

The hymn by St. Francis of Assisi is a translation by William Draper, copyright by G. Curwen and Sons. Used by permission of G. Shirmer, Inc.

Quotations from the *Bhagavad-Gita* are from the translation by Swami Prabhavananda and Christopher Isherwood, published by The New American Library, copyright held by Vedanta Society of Southern California. Used by permission.

Quotations from *The Religions of Man* by Huston Smith are by permission of Harper and Row Publishers.

The quotation on Ju-jutsu by Alan Watts. is printed by permission of Grove Press, Inc, where the 1958 copyright is held.

Poems quoted from the *Tao Te Ching* are from the R.B. Blakney; translation entitled *The Way of Life: Lao Tzu* published by The New American Library.

Quotations from *Between God and Man* by Abraham Joshua Heschel are used by permission of Macmillan Publishing Company.

Quotations from *This is My God* by Herman Wouk are used by permission of the author.

The two poems from *Songs from the Slums* by Toyohiko Kagawa are used by permission of Abingdon Press (copyright renewal 1963 by Lois J. Erickson.)

The lines from surah 96 of the Koran are from *The Meaning of the Glorious Koran* translated by Mohammed Marmaduke Pickthall, published by the New American Library.

Quotations from the *Autobiography of Malcolm X* are used by permission of Grove Press, Inc.

The story "Flower" in the Appendix is from *Deep Well* by Emil Paul John, used by permission of Friendship Press. The other story in the Appendix, "Gohei Saves his Village," is from *Fun and Festival from Japan* published by permission of Friendship Press.

Biblical quotations throughout this book are largely from the Revised Standard Version Bible, published by 1952 by Thomas Nelson and Sons. Used by permission.

* * * * *

Statistics on numbers of followers of various religions are rounded out from the 1974 *World Almanac*, page 342.

Photo Credits

Pg. 16 —Maryknoll
Pg. 27 —Maryknoll
Pg. 28 —Press Information Bureau/Government of India at New Delhi
Pg. 34 —Maryknoll
Pg. 46 —*(left)* James P. Colligan, Maryknoll *(right)* Embassy of Sri-Lanka
Pg. 50 —William J. Stravitz, Maryknoll
Pg. 62 —Maryknoll
Pg. 66 —Israel Ministry of Tourism
Pg. 79 —Israel Ministry of Tourism
Pg. 81 —*(top)* Religion Teacher's Journal *(bottom)* Fred Baemer
Pg. 86 —Twenty-Third Publications
Pg. 101—Religious News Service
Pg. 102—Paul M. Schrock
Pg. 106—Iran Information & Tourism Center
Pg. 118—Royal Embassy of Saudi Arabia; *(l.l.)* Religious News Service

Artwork: Maryann Read and Ed Curley

Cover design: Dan Johnson—Art Direction, Inc.